The Man with Six Typewriters

The Man with Six Typewriters

...and Others Who Knew God

Steve Doughty

Foreword by Jane E. Vennard

To Elizabeth...
With gratitude for your
abiding friendship and for all
your encouragement in the
formation of the pages that
follow...

Steve

WIPF & STOCK · Eugene, Oregon

THE MAN WITH SIX TYPEWRITERS
. . . and Others Who Knew God

Wipf & Stock
An Imprint of Wipf and Stock Publishers
199 W. 8th Ave., Suite 3
Eugene, OR 97401

www.wipfandstock.com

ISBN 13: 978-1-4982-1849-8

Manufactured in the U.S.A.   03/09/2015

Poems by Mīzrā 'Abd al-Qādir Bīdal and Muhammad Shams al-Dīn Hīfiz
are from the book *Love's Alchemy*. Copyright © 2006 by David and Sabrineh Fideler. Reprinted with permission of New World Library, Novato,
CA. www.newworldlibrary.com

The story "How beautiful you are, my love . . ." was first published online
by *Rock and Sling*, November, 2010. rockandsling.com

Unless otherwise noted all Scripture quotations contained herein are from
the New Revised Standard Version of the Bible, copyright © 1989 by the
Division of Christian Education of the National Council of Churches in
the U.S.A. and are used by permission. All rights reserved. The one varia-
tion from this is, as noted in the text, from the Revised Standard Version
of the Bible, copyright © 1952 by the Division of Christian Education of
the National Council of the Churches of Christ in the United States of
America, used by permission. All rights reserved.

For
Elliott and Caroline

God is love, and those who abide in love abide in God,
and God abides in them.

I JOHN 4:16B

Here and there amid the arid hills of human experience are well-springs
and fountain-heads of religious intuition. They are the original source of all
religion. They need not always be of great grandeur. They may be humble
rivulets of feeling. Or, they may give rise to great rivers of refreshment
flowing through the centuries. But always, great or small, they bear upon
themselves the stamp of their own authenticity.[1]

W. T. STACE
TIME AND ETERNITY

You see Alice over there? My wife, forty-seven years. I tell you, she's a saint!
And do you see my neighbor Timmie? Same thing!

AN AGING VERMONTER

1. Stace, *Time and Eternity*, 3.

Contents

Foreword

Jane E. Vennard

As I READ THROUGH Steve Doughty's beautifully written stories I began to realize that these were more than essays, more than narratives. They were touching something deep inside me. When I came across the quote from fourteenth century Persian poet Hāfiz who wrote "love existed before heaven and earth,"[1] I realized I was reading a book of love letters.

It is clear that Steve loves the women and men and children who are celebrated in this book and he wants his readers to love them as well. They include the elderly and the young at heart, the talkative and the silent ones. Some are confused; others grieving; many finding joy. All of them are a testimony to the resilience of the human spirit in difficult and puzzling situations.

Steve does not shy away from the realities of the world. His stories include war, hatred, poverty, and death. And within that context he is able to hold the tension between the dark and the light, ugliness and beauty, death and life. Steve explores the complexity of being alive in a multifaceted world.

In one of my favorite stories, *Umbrella Moment*, Steve describes how he and his wife Jean greeted and spoke with a Muslim family of six at a peace vigil in their hometown. As people gathered in a park the looming clouds suddenly opened and sheets of rain poured down upon them. Steve and Jean had a large umbrella that

---

1. Fedeler and Fedeler, *Love's Alchemy*, v.

they offered to the family who pressed together forming a single, lumpy knot under the protective canopy.

The mother motioned for Jean and Steve to join them making a knot of eight. There was no more than an inch or two between the adult's faces and children's heads pressed into their bellies and thighs. From this huddle they heard the woman's voice asking, "Isn't this really what peace vigils are all about?"

Soon after that holy moment the rain stopped as abruptly as it had begun. Umbrellas came down and suddenly into the silence harsh angry voices began shouting hatred and violence. The gathering for peace was overcome by toxic hate-filled forces causing people to flee. In reflection Steve explores the pain and discouragement of such paradoxical moments at the same time finding hope. He writes, "Her sharing was swiftly crushed, but in that moment under the umbrella she dared point to something new."

The possibility of something new emerges as a theme that Steve often strengthens by the thoughts and words of other writers who you realize have informed and formed him over the years. He calls on ancient and modern theologians, saints and mystics from many religious traditions, scientists, essayists, and poets. They serve both Steve and the reader in reflecting on the experiences of others, but never do these words of wisdom take center stage, for always the person is at the heart of the story.

These persons are real people who Steve met by chance, such as the Muslim family under the umbrella, or through his experiences of being a pastor. He is the narrator who does not hesitate to claim his place in the stories, but never makes them about himself. Steve has found the unique place in the craft of writing that allows the narrator to be in the story and to speak in the first person while pointing away from himself and back to the one who is the person whom he has encountered.

Even in the story *Supplicant,* that begins with Steve and Jean hearing from his father that his mother's brain tumor is inoperable, the story is not about them but about Jack, a friend who shows up to pray with them in the midst of their grief. Jack's prayer was rough and hesitant as he searched for words. The simple words he found revealed his sincerity and faithfulness. Steve goes on to reflect on the meaning of prayer in his own life and in others. But the reflections lead back to Jack who Steve describes leaving their house that night with his head down and barely uttering a word. He concludes that story with these words of wonder about the presence of Jack in their lives in their time of brokenness and despair – "In our presence, he had dared approach the Holy."

Holiness is another theme that runs through the stories in this collection. It may be glimpsed in relationships that include touch, laughter, tears, and dancing. In other places within the book the focus is on the holiness of creation and the joy of those who are able to perceive it. The man at the center of *Stargazer* gets up every morning at 5 a.m. to look on line at the "Hubble Telescope" and shares his excitement with Steve at their weekly breakfasts. They don't try to understand what has been seen; they simply rest in awe and mystery.

Mystery is celebrated throughout this book. Steve is not trying to convince the reader of anything. He is not attempting to answer questions that have not been asked. His purpose is to share with us the mystery and holiness of the human experience as seen through his eyes and heart.

The Man with Six Typewriters is a wholehearted book. The characters come alive, and it seemed to me as if I were making new friends. I often felt I was there with Steve in the coffee shop or in a person's living room, at the church or on the streets. Reader, beware! Your heart may be broken open and new ways revealed as you encounter the holiness in the midst of ordinary life.

Rev. Jane E Vennard, author of *Fully Awake and Truly Alive: Spiritual Practices to Nurture Your Soul (2013)* and *Teaching—The Sacred Art: The Joy of Opening Minds and Hearts (2015)*

Acknowledgments

IN TWO OF THE churches where I led studies of the manuscript for this book I was asked politely, "Are we guinea pigs?" The only honest answer I could come up with was, "The best!" The churches varied in their setting, membership, and even theological outlook. They shared the same last name, that being Presbyterian, plus, in the groups I met with, the capacity to ask probing questions and offer affirmation in the same breath. So to study groups at North Park and Westminster, in Grand Rapids, Michigan, and John Knox, Fourth, and Westminster in Greenville, South Carolina, I extend my heartfelt thanks for shaping and sharpening this entire work. For conversations that shall always be with me and relate to much that follows in this book, I extend similar thanks to Mary Budde and Ray Diffenderfer, Pat Shufeldt, Carl Ill, Fred Cunningham, Dick Jackson, Nelson Lumm, Gene and Penny Jennings, Doris and Richard Strife, Catherine Powell, Ruth Noel, Shoray Kirk, Tom Fallaw, George Donigian, Ferdie Hintze, Shirley Souder, Delcy Khulman, Sr. Elizabeth Smoyer, and for the generous offer of their cabin for a much needed time of reflection, Don and Debbie Fontaine. At the Collegeville Institute, Collegeville, Minnesota, I received essential counsel from Executive Director Don Ottenhoff and deeply valued encouragement from the community of resident scholars during the early phases of writing. I wish to express special thanks to Lynne Deming for her outstanding editorial work on the final manuscript, and to Davis Taylor, poet and friend, whose sensitive observations on this entire project have come as an immense gift. Lastly, and most of all, my thanks to Jean. Her wisdom, humor, insights, and encouragement have been of help beyond measure through every step in gathering and now sharing the stories that follow.

Introduction

Sometimes a person needs a story more than food to stay alive.[1]

BARRY LOPEZ

THE PEOPLE ON THE following pages have fed my soul with their stories. Among them are a Muslim woman and Christian couple meeting at a peace vigil, a miner receiving his last communion, a Native American stone carver, a minister dazzled by photos from the Hubble telescope, and two attorneys risking their lives to defend victims of political violence in Colombia, South America. These persons have lived out their tales in such disparate places as the St. Lawrence River Valley, the Black Hills of South Dakota, Appalachia, the middle-sized city of Kalamazoo, and coastal Colombia. They never said, "Let me tell you about myself." They shared their stories the way most people do. They lived. And I, sometimes as a pastor who knew them well, sometimes as a stranger suddenly aware of them nearby, got to watch.

These persons speak to my longing for authenticity. When I call them to mind, I encounter neither hype nor pat answers. I see people who contend unceremoniously with life and faith. They search, struggle, and quietly persevere. Some laugh or, half on purpose I am sure, present the rest of us with the opportunity to laugh at ourselves.

1. Lopez, *Crow and Weasel*, 48.

An early observer of these stories offered, "You won't find many of these people seated at the 'head table.'" That is true. A fair number have never even seen the inside of a banquet hall. They include the unnoticed, the marginalized. The few privileged ones among them remain down-to-earth. They hold low visibility in common, plus one more element. In the earthiness of their lives, in their pain and laughter and plodding along, they speak of God. They tell of The Holy in our midst. Some do this directly with a few words or even a whole sentence. More often they become God's messengers through the stuff of their daily lives. Some of these messengers stand outside the Christian faith that was formative for me as a child and remains at the core of my life. Christian or not, poor or not, "head table" candidates or not, all feast on life's multi-layered abundance in an age hungering to rediscover what life is about. The feast they have discovered may look spare by the world's standards, but that doesn't matter. The world leaves out too much, and these people would choose no other way.

In the stories that follow nobody makes pious pronouncements about God. No one passes along a slip of paper saying, "Here is the moral to my story." These persons tender a subtler gift. They offer images to ponder. Images of real people. Images of the wonderings and affirmations that take place within our deepest selves. And, finally, images of the living God at work within us, among us, and through us. As with all such images, these challenge us at least as much as they comfort and reassure.

I have two hopes as I share these stories. The first is that I will be forgiven for what I have left out. Countless other stories could accompany those offered here. I have made selections to accent variety and even to play with it. God beckons us in realms as varied as the aching quest for justice, the arts and sciences, sexuality, and the humdrum pattern of daily life. In honoring this variety I have neglected additional tales from each realm. Further, from the stories that follow I have probably eliminated too much. In some instances I have altered names. At times I have accented a specific line of narration to highlight particular facets of what was going on. This editing has invariably left other matters in the shadows or not visible at all. So I ask mercy for what is lacking.

My second hope is that the figures in these stories will do for readers what they have done for me and for others with whom I have shared their narratives. I hope they will invite readers to a greater awareness. To be aware is to be cognizant. It is to be watchful. In its deepest sense, to be aware is to be alive. A good poem awakens us to subtleties of life and spirit we too often hurry past. We finish reading the poem, but then the poem is not done with us. It continues to open our eyes. A good novel does the same, and so can a song or a dance. So can a life fully lived, no matter how humble, daring, pain-filled, or seemingly humdrum that life is. The lives shared in this book invite us to look at what they are finding and to join, wide-eyed, in the discovery.

The Appendix to this book contains questions that have proven helpful to individuals and groups engaged in study or retreat with these stories. Some persons may wish to turn to these pages. Doubtless, readers will come up with their own questions as well. Further, I am sure that on encountering these narratives readers will recall stories of which this writer knows nothing at all. To that I simply say, "Good!" When Gerard Manley Hopkins wrote, "The world is charged with the grandeur of God,"[2] he was absolutely right. That grandeur lives down the street. It sits across the table from us. If we dare admit it, we may see the divine grandeur break forth when we trace, in even the simplest places, the storied paths of our own lives.

Steve Doughty
Epiphany, 2015

---

2. Hopkins, *Gerard Manley Hopkins*, 27.

1

The Man with Six Typewriters

HENRY HAD TYPED THE Bible seventeen times when we met. Genesis 1:1 right through Revelation 22:21. From "In the beginning" to that final "The grace of the Lord Jesus be with all the saints. Amen." He even put in the individual verse numbers. For copying, he favored the Revised Standard Version, though he also liked the King James and, on occasion, the Living Bible Paraphrased. Somewhere along the line he got two of his typed editions formally bound. Across the top of the first page in one he had written firmly, "Please God, forgive me for any mistakes I have made here."

Henry was in his mid-sixties the year a friend introduced us. When he was just a boy growing up in Appalachia, he and his mother were in an auto accident. She was killed instantly. He spent months recovering. Within a year relatives began to say, "he's going mental." Ultimately he was diagnosed with a complex of mental disorders that he learned to live with and manage, but they never fully left him. As a young man he moved to Indianapolis for work, but employment proved difficult. At one point he spent three years in a state mental hospital. It was there he started typing the Bible. "It helped me keep my focus," he said. Eventually he made his way up to Michigan.

The scripture copying habit did not prevent Henry from enjoying life. One afternoon I went to see him at the nursing home where he spent his last years. He and another fellow sat out in the hallway, bent over and grinning like two kids who were both winning at marbles.

"You guys look happy."

They glanced at each other, then stared down at their hands. Neither said a word.

"Hmm?" I said.

Another pause. Then from Henry, quite matter of fact, "We found out we sort of liked the same woman once." The man next to him twitched his shoulders. Henry's eyes glowed. He started to giggle.

This conversation did not need a third party. "Well, I'll see you later."

"Thanks!" said Henry.

Typing the Bible, though, remained important after Henry entered the nursing home. Or at least the hope that he might do it again remained important. When living on his own, Henry had invited me over to his apartment. It was a simple two-room affair in a run-down subsidized complex built back in the 1960s. I no sooner got through the door than I spotted a Smith Corona sitting on his kitchen table. I complimented him. "Nice machine."

"I've got five more! Two under the bed and three in the closet. All of them electric." He was proud and invited me to look under the bed. The two were stored neatly, in keeping with everything else in the apartment. "If one goes on the blink, I've always got another. Trouble is keeping them repaired. It costs."

We sat at the kitchen table. The Smith Corona had a sheet of colored paper in it, typed down to the halfway point with words from the prophet Micah. As I left, Henry introduced me to his tank of guppies. For my benefit as much as theirs, he fed them. "They're the only living thing they let you keep in this place. I like 'em."

When he moved to the nursing home, the guppies weren't allowed and there was no space for the typewriters. The home had a large tank of tropical fish in the dining area, so he enjoyed that, but Henry grieved the loss of his writing machines. His caseworker got concerned about depression and one day showed up with an aging but functional Remington. Since Henry had few visitors, the two agreed it could sit on the chair by his bed. The next time I stopped, Henry proudly introduced me to his new friend.

The typewriter stayed next to him for a year. When he switched rooms, it got put on a corner table. Finally it wound up in a closet. The plain truth was, from the very start Henry couldn't use it. "Dang!" was his strongest pronouncement on the situation. His fingers no longer did what he wanted them to, even when nurses put the typewriter on a solid surface and set him in a good position to try.

Other matters began to fill his days. For the first time since his years in the state hospital, Henry found himself surrounded by large numbers of people. Wheelchair bound, he cruised the halls. He went on outings and bus trips when given the chance. Most of all, he began to learn names. Names of residents. Names of staff. Names of volunteers. Names were his new keyboard and he learned to hit the right one every time. "Hi Jeff!" "Hi, Sara!" "Hello, Mr. VanHecke."

Henry's roommates tended to move out or die off in quick order. After two years Fred turned up in the next bed. He was a retired cab driver and the two had known each other years before. Fred had pancreatic cancer. One look at him and it was clear that his stay with Henry would be brief.

Henry reached out first. Fred responded and the two cared for each other as best they could. Fred chatted and told old stories. Henry listened, and he rang the bell at night if Fred needed help. "That Henry, he's a good one," Fred chirped to me in their sixth week.

One morning I walked in and Fred was having a particularly difficult time. He asked that I untangle his top sheet and spread it so he could roll over without exposing himself. I fluffed the sheet. He tried to turn, yelled, and asked for a pain killer. Two nurses hurried in. They tended to him behind drawn curtains while I visited with Henry. We heard more cries of pain and then, still louder, "I'm dizzy!" Henry called back "Hang on, old buddy!" The nurses were still working with Fred, who was moaning, when I had to go. As I headed out the door, Fred heard me going and topped all his earlier sounds with "Thanks for the prayer. You have a good day!" He meant it. That was the last time I heard his voice.

Two months later Henry began his own steady decline. It went on for nearly two years, but from the start the direction was unmistakable. A trip to the hospital. Then another. Stays of a few days, then of a week, then of weeks at a time. Heart and lung failure. Diabetes. Back and forth between the advancing illnesses.

All the while I heard from hospital staff members, "He is the sweetest man" and "What a fine person." Of course one half expects such things, but the comments were in earnest and beyond the usual. "Even when we don't feel well, he gives us joy." "He greets us each by name." "He always says 'thanks!'" "He helps me stay whole."

As I walked back to the hospital parking lot one day, I mused on hearing "He is the sweetest man" for what must have been the fiftieth time. My mind moved to another use of the word "sweet." I half dismissed the thought as it took shape, but it rattled around in my head all the way home. Ages ago, Ezekiel was commanded to eat a scroll. The scroll was the divine word. And the word tasted as sweet as honey.[1]

Seventeen times Henry had typed the Bible. For all his efforts over the past few years he deserved honorary credit for the eighteenth. Through his persistent pounding of the keys had he managed to absorb some ethereal yet now unmistakable sweetness? Of course there had been bitterness to sort through, things like psalms of vengeance and cursing and babies' heads getting bashed against the stones. But what might Henry have taken within? What of still waters? What about love for the neighbor? What of spiritual fruits like kindness, patience, gentleness, and self-control? He never said a word about any of this. He never even mentioned why he chose the Bible in the first place. Why not *The New York Times* or *Outdoor Life*? Henry didn't make pronouncements. He just did

---

1. Ezekiel 3:3.

his work. That afternoon, though, I wondered. What had gone on with this work?

Not long after this, I received the expected call. It came at 1 a.m. Henry was on hospice now and back at the nursing home. The voice on the other end of the line informed me that his blood-oxygen level had just dropped to seventy. I drove twenty miles to the home. A night aide I'd never seen before welcomed me and took me into his room. "They just don't make them like this guy any more," she said. Then she went back down the hall, ready to usher in the hospice nurse who had been called.

Henry breathed unevenly. An hour passed.

The nurse arrived. She checked his blood oxygen. It was up to seventy-five. In accord with Henry's instructions, nobody was doing anything to keep him going. At 3:30 a.m. the level had risen to eighty-five. I went home to rest.

Early in the afternoon I returned to the nursing home. Henry's room was empty. Figuring what had happened, I walked out to the nursing station. "Henry died?" I said. "Oh no," answered the nurse. "His blood-ox went up to ninety-five. Amazing. He wanted to go out and see people, and we figured 'Why not?'"

I found him in his wheelchair at the far end of the home, greeting anybody he saw as he chugged along.

Henry died three months later. His service was simple, just as he wished.

Not long afterward, two events occurred. They were inter-related, though the nature of that relation defies precise articulation. For both, it is important to note that a few years before we met, Henry was hit by a truck and became permanently lame. In restitution, the trucking firm paid him sixty-thousand dollars. For somebody poor and suffering chronic mental illness, this was a lot. He gave a portion to some relatives. He prepaid his funeral so nobody else would have to bother. With the help of his case worker, he made the rest last as long as he could, giving to charity and putting a modest percentage into typewriters.

The first event came in the form of a letter from the nursing home where he died. On opening it, I could see that some

well-intentioned soul had made the mistake I'd been trying to cor-
rect for two years. Because I had durable power of attorney for
health care for Henry, some thought I was linked to him financially, but I was not. The letter said the home wanted to be sure I
received all of Henry's remaining personal wealth. Attached was a
check for thirty-five cents.

The second event came a few weeks later when I drove to the
cemetery to see if Henry's marker was in place. I hunted for a time
as the cemetery was large, and though I had been present for his
service, I lost my way. At length I came upon the smallest, freshest
stone in the park. It was dark granite, flush to the ground, nothing
obtrusive. Just what he wanted. It bore his name, his dates, and in
the upper right hand corner an open Bible with "The Lord is my
shepherd" deeply incised across both pages.

2

Two Marked Attorneys

[In the first nine years of the new millennium 4 million Colombians were forced from their land by crop fumigation and armed violence. The displaced, amounting to nearly ten percent of Colombia's population, were disproportionately of African and Indigenous heritage and almost entirely from rural areas where the land moved rapidly from ownership by farming families to control by multi-national corporations and a few wealthy Colombians.

During Lent, 2009, through the Peace Fellowship of the Presbyterian Church (U.S.A.), I joined friend and translator Ruth Noel in accompanying members of the Iglesia Presbiteriana de Colombia as they worked for human rights in the midst of an increasingly dangerous situation. At this time we met Juana and Jorge. For obvious reasons, I share neither their true names nor precisely where they lived.]

Juana

It was 9:45 a.m. The temperature had already hit ninety-five degrees and the air had thickened in a sprawling Colombian city of over one million people. No clouds. Ruth Noel and I were pressed tightly in the back of a small cab. Next to the driver sat our host and indefatigable guide, Alejandro, an Elder of the Iglesia Presbiteriana de Colombia. Alejandro had arranged the meeting we were having at ten o'clock. "She's an attorney. You will want to hear her," was all he had said a few days before. The cab bucked its way through narrow streets crowded with pedestrians, motor scooters, burro-drawn wagons, and other cars trying to press their way through the ever-shifting mass.

"¡Pare!" Alejandro called. This was the first word the normally garrulous man spoke on the trip. The cab slammed to a halt.

We got out, said nothing, and followed Alejandro as he had instructed, looking neither to the left nor the right.

He led us swiftly up the steps to a two-story cement building. We passed through an open door and found ourselves face-to-face with a guard in military uniform seated behind a desk. Alejandro said we had an appointment with Juana. The guard looked each of us up and down, said nothing, and gave a heavy nod towards a stairway behind him.

Bars covered every door and window we passed on the second story. None of the offices appeared open. Alejandro stopped in front of one door, reached through the bars and knocked. Ruth and I looked in the window. No lights shone inside. We could make out a small room, an open door to a room beyond that, and what appeared to be a third room beyond that. Alejandro knocked again. A shadowed form appeared from the back room, stepped to the front, undid the lock, and waved us in.

We followed the woman into the second room where she switched on an overhead light. She signaled for us to sit in three white, plastic chairs arranged in front of her desk. The office was simple. Two small pictures hung on the wall. The floor space was completely taken by the plastic chairs, a modest desk, a computer, printer, and one file cabinet of the same design as others we could now see lining the walls of the third room.

"Bienvienidos," the woman said, with just a slight smile. "Soy Juana." Ruth and I spoke our names. Juana was young and athletic, her darkened skin and thick black hair suggesting a blend of Indigenous South American and African backgrounds. In the next hour she kept steady eye contact with all three of us, including me, even though it was clear from Ruth's ongoing, whispered translation that I needed help to understand her.

She wanted to start with a little history. She worked for the Committee for Solidarity with Political Prisoners, a non-government organization founded in the early 1970s to protect the rights of political prisoners.

"There was a strike," Juana said. "The government sent in troops and crushed it. Lawyers met with laboring people to see how they could support them." Out of this, the organization she worked for was born. Its attorneys did pro bono work for people falsely accused. They also dealt with the civil rights of prisoners, both political and non-political. Juana and the other attorneys currently operated six major offices around Colombia and six smaller ones, but these offices were not nearly enough to handle all the cases.

Juana shifted her focus to the specifics of imprisonment. The office we sat in related to four prisons in the region. One, completed with U.S. dollars through Plan Colombia, was modeled after maximum-security prisons in the United States. "The human rights abuses there are massive," Juana noted. "Families can visit only once every three months. Prisoners are beaten. The food quality is terrible." There had been deaths from food contaminated by bacteria. She knew prisoners who had gone for days without water.

"When people finally get to visit, there is much harassment. They must pass through lots of doors, and wait an hour at each one." A recent law allowed people to visit labor leaders only if they could obtain an order from the judge who ruled in the case.

All of this Juana spoke quietly. She looked at each of us as she offered what she was encountering. She never raised her voice or clenched a fist. She let what she shared speak for itself.

The maximum-security prison could hold a thousand prisoners. Its current population was 1,485. Another ten such prisons were planned. These were to be built with U.S. dollars. The population was projected to be over two thousand in each.

The telephone rang and Juana took the call. Alejandro leaned toward Ruth and me. "Did you see the guard when we came in? The security system has been put here by the government. It's not here for Juana's safety. The government wants to know everyone who comes to see her. It is one more means of intimidation." A Colombian newspaper had recently run stories on the government's wiretapping of human rights advocates.

Juana continued on the phone.

I had a chance to study the two pictures on the wall. The one behind her desk could have hung in any campus dorm I knew back in the 1960s. A goofy looking guy wearing suspenders but no shirt popped out of a tire and grimaced at anybody glancing at the photo. I turned to the other photo, off to the side of the desk, close and at eye level for Juana. A young man stood behind a podium. He wore glasses, was handsome, trim, and had high cheekbones and dark hair combed tight to his head. He raised a muscular arm as he spoke to a crowd gathered before him.

Juana finished her phone conversation. She shifted to the plight of labor leaders who were seeking to help the poor. They were falsely accused of siding with the guerillas, which they did not, but because of the accusations they were subject to imprisonment. When imprisoned they faced heightened restrictions on the number of family visits they could receive in a year. Common criminals could go free after serving sixty percent of their assigned time. Labor leaders had to serve eighty percent. When finally eligible, they were required to pay a fine set so high that they could not afford it.

Juana shared figures Ruth and I had heard before. In the preceding year, at least forty-two Colombian labor leaders were assassinated. The government responded saying that a war was going on and some people were bound to be killed. Of the 1174 trade unionists murdered throughout the world between 1999 and 2005, over eight hundred were Colombian. Of these, 416 were teachers who called attention to the economic, social, and cultural rights of ordinary citizens.

The hour had passed. Juana had cases to attend to. As we stood, she thanked us for coming. I gestured to the pictures on the wall. "These?" I said.

She ignored the guy in the tire and turned towards the young man behind the podium. "He was a labor leader and spoke for people's rights," she said. "He was accused of being a guerilla, which he was not. He was tortured. He was killed."

Juana led us quietly to the door. We walked downstairs and past the guard who knew her every move and contact.

Jorge

Two days after we met Juana, Ruth and I sat on a bench awaiting Jorge's arrival outside a small room provided for him by a group of Presbyterian churches. A couple came up. "Is Jorge in?" the woman asked. Hearing "Not yet," they joined us on the bench. The woman looked to be around fifty, the man far older. They held hands.

Unbidden, the woman told their story. In 2000 they were forced off land they had owned and worked since their marriage many years before. By law, as *displacazados,* they were entitled to monetary compensation, health care, and education for the three teen-age children living with them at the time. After an eight-year delay the government acknowledged that, yes, they were displaced. Just a week ago, after further delays, papers arrived entitling them to their financial compensation. The woman had taken the papers to the bank as directed.

"Oh," the banker had said, "we can't give you the money. You already signed for it." He showed her a large book. Somebody had signed her name, though not in her hand, and given her thumb-print, though it wasn't her thumb.

"You have to tell your President what is happening to us!" the woman said. "He is not getting the full story. We have no money, no work. New families arrive at our camp all the time. One new family is living under a tree. We are treated very badly."

At this point Jorge arrived. He apologized to the couple for being late. He asked Ruth and me if we could wait until the next day.

The following afternoon the three of us met, as Jorge suggested, on a balcony overlooking a school courtyard. He immediately brought up the couple we had seen the day before. "What they experienced has happened thousands of times," he said. "It is always the same. Somebody high up knows these people will be coming, so the money is signed for and gone by the time they get there. They have already lost everything. They live in extreme poverty. Now this happens to them." Jorge had filed a legal complaint but expected little to come of it.

Jorge had a young family to support and a fledgling legal practice. He spent hours each week volunteering to advocate for persons whose rights had been violated. Jorge and his organization sought national and international attention for the violations taking place. They were now compiling a data bank on the eight million human rights violations over the past ten years. The head of this project, a highly respected Jesuit priest, had been charged with criminal activity by the government. The leader of the entire organization had been accused of being a subversive and jailed for six months. Death threats had forced another young attorney to leave the country.

Jorge turned to a discussion of *falsos positivos*. For years the army paid bonuses to soldiers who killed guerillas. And for years young men had been disappearing from poor neighborhoods in Colombian cities. Human rights workers long suspected that many bodies of guerillas were actually "false positives," men who never had anything to do with guerilla activity. In November 2008, it came to light that seventeen men in a Bogotá barrio were offered work, driven into the jungle, and murdered by the army. Papers identifying them as guerillas were then placed on their bodies. Following this revelation, one of Colombia's top generals was relieved of his command. Just three weeks later, President Uribe appointed him Ambassador to the Dominican Republic.

Jorge shook his head. He noted that sixty bodies had recently been discovered in a mass grave. Could these be false positives? "Nobody has claimed the bodies. There is such fear out there." Jorge fell silent.

"Your courage," Ruth asked, "where do you find the courage to keep dealing with all this?"

"The courage? The courage is there because we believe in God." His words were soft. "As followers of Jesus we are accountable." And then he quoted Paul in his letter to the Philippians, "I can do all things through him who strengthens me." His answer was as direct as his passion for the violated.

After a moment he went further. He had to admit that he had thought about leaving the work. He worried for his family. He wanted more time with his wife and children. The whole situation was very hard. "But then I am with people like the two you saw yesterday. They have nobody to represent them. Their need is so real. My energy comes back. I cannot stop."

At this point a voice called "Jorge!" from below the balcony. We looked down and saw a weathered man in a torn t-shirt and old khaki pants. Jorge smiled and beckoned him up. It was time for Ruth and me to go.

In the days following our meetings with Juana and Jorge, I found myself reflecting on how marked these two attorneys were. They were marked by the government, marked by threatening, even lethal forces that feared the light they shed. They were marked too by the pain of others around them. And they were marked most profoundly by the same eternal stirring that not long ago broke into our world saying, "I have a dream!" and ages past sounded through the voice of a beleaguered prophet of God's justice for the poor who in anguish cried:

> If I say "I will not mention him,
>   or speak any more in his name,"
> then within me there is something like a burning fire

shut up in my bones;
    I am weary with holding it in,
        and I cannot.

JEREMIAH 20:9

Juana and Jorge are so marked, branded. Whatever may have happened to them, they still speak.

3

Stargazer

As long as the drop
hadn't emerged from the sea
the ocean
didn't notice
the depths of its splendor.[1]

MĪZRĀ 'ABD AL-QĀDIR BĪDIL
EIGHTEENTH CENTURY C. E.

MY FRIEND HAD CLAIMED our traditional booth at Panera Bread when I arrived at 7:10 a.m. I said "Hi," got my tea and muffin, came back, and lurched into my side of the booth. He shoved a sheet of paper in front of me.

"Just look at that!" He slapped his hand down by the paper. In the middle of the page I saw a swirling haze four inches in diameter. Explosions of red, pink, orange, and green surged outward in all directions from a fiery white center. Here and there blue beams of light pierced the vibrating form along its edge. The entire scene lay on a pillow of darkness.

1. Fideler and Fideler, *Love's Alchemy*, 51.

"Here!" he said, and thrust a forefinger at a small arc of light pressing towards the right side of the page. For a moment his finger slipped over the entire arc, then he pulled it back. "Do you know how big that is? It takes a year for light to travel from one end of that tiny line to the other. And this cloud you are looking at?" He boxed the swirling form between his hands. "It's sixteen light years across. It takes sixteen years for light to get from one side of this cloud to the other!"

"There!" he pointed near the center of the page. "They've found a disk that could turn into another solar system. And here!" He hit his hand on the whiteness. "Here hundreds of stars are being born."

He leaned back in the booth. "I can't believe it!"

For two years he had subjected himself to this kind of exhilaration every morning except Sundays. Faithfully he would get up at 5 a.m., shuffle to his computer, click on "Hubble Telescope," and pull up a cosmic photo for the day. Then he would sit and gaze at it. His ensuing enthusiasm was one of the many reasons I enjoyed our breakfasts. Today was the first time he brought a picture.

In the preceding months he had offered a number of other excitements, all of the scientific variety. "Have you heard that scientists are increasingly convinced that time arose out of something that has nothing to do with time?"[2] Well, no, I had to say. I could not recall a single conversation during the preceding week where that had come up.

"Astrophysicists are exploring how time may have arisen from a dimension that knows no time," he continued. "Isn't that exciting?!"

It was 7:15 a.m. Any form of excitement was tough. Yet even apart from the theology I cherish, which suggests time exists in the wider and barely understandable realm of eternity, this was provocative. I had to admit, yes, this was exciting. And mind-stretching.

One morning he came in chuckling. The night before he had read an essay by Owen Gingerich, Professor Emeritus of

2. Lanier, "Raft to the Future," *Discover Magazine* online.

Astronomy and the History of Science at Harvard. Gingerich noted that British astronomer Fred Hoyle found his atheism "deeply shaken" when predictions he had made on the unique properties of the carbon nucleus proved to be true. Without those finely tuned properties there would be no life as we know it.[3] My friend was not laughing at Hoyle. Nor was he, like some others, gleefully latching onto Hoyle's reaction as instant proof of some tightly fashioned "intelligent design." For the moment he simply laughed at what he called "the absolute wonder and miracle that we are here at all!"

On another occasion he arrived with eyes wide. It seemed that Islamic mystical designs of the fifteenth century had perfectly prefigured concepts just now discovered by modern mathematicians.[4] That morning my friend's only pronouncement was, "How is it that the depths of science and mysticism come together?"

Today, though, he was absorbed by the exploding form on the paper before him. He just sat and looked at it. He made no more gestures. Neither of us said a word.

I looked at him as he gazed downward. How many knew him in this way? I had seen him in the pulpit. A lot. He ministered to a small congregation at the poorer end of his city. Half the people worshiping each Sunday lived with chronic mental illness. I had encountered him and his wife standing in line at peace vigils. Periodically he wrote pieces in the newspaper calling attention to the needs of the mentally ill or supporting the rights of those discriminated against because of their sexual orientation. Such work was public. His scientific explorations and enthusiasms were more private.

"I wish we had words for this" he said, looking up from the picture. "All the energy, the beauty, all the eons and eons of time. Look at what science is showing us! Our church language doesn't fit anymore. God sitting up there, looking down and saying, 'Let this happen' and 'Let that happen.' That was fine once, but it's too cramped a vision. The reality outstrips all our images. We're stuck

---

3. Gingerich, *God's Universe*, 56–57.
4. Prang, "Tiles of Infinity," 24–31.

in the Middle Ages with a three-story universe. God is absolutely in all of this, but how do we even begin to portray it?"

He had asked this half a dozen times before. He knew I didn't have an answer.

His forefinger tapped the swirling nebula. "Beautiful," he said. Then he pushed the paper aside.

"Thomas," he continued. "I see Thomas tonight."

Thomas had a low IQ, battled depression, and occasionally got in trouble with the police for picking up people's wallets at the public library. He had lived on his own for five years. Half the renters in his apartment complex were hooked on drugs. My friend took Thomas bowling twice a month. He never knew what he'd find when he went to pick him up.

"Two weeks ago he was horribly depressed," my friend said. "His shades were drawn tight. He was hardly eating. His case worker was involved, but oh, the pain of depression is excruciating. It just goes on and on."

Thomas had nothing to do with my friend's church. He wasn't likely to.

"Why do you keep seeing him?" I asked.

"His courage moves me. Besides, I like him."

A men's Bible study began at the table next to our booth. It was Wednesday, 7:30 a.m. We had forgotten. We usually met for breakfast on Thursdays and when we did hit Wednesdays the Bible group met on the far side of the room. Not so today.

My friend tried to draw me out on what was happening in my own life, but conversation became difficult as the Bible study was getting loud. Well, not the Bible study as a whole. Only the minister in charge. He had a voice that could make God jealous, and he wasn't about to cut it back just because he was in a restaurant instead of the pulpit. We had experienced his resonance previously, but having him parked right next to us created a whole new set of sensations. Not all of these were conducive to serious discourse.

We didn't eaves-drop. On the other hand, we didn't plug our ears as that would have run the risk of serious misinterpretation on the part of the minister reading out loud from the Bible. I was sure that inwardly my friend and I agreed the minister was superbly prepared. He had a large number of carefully worded questions. Not only that. He had answers for every one of them. Extensive answers. Answers that sent the young men in his tutelage flipping from verses in the front of the Bible to verses near the middle of the Bible and then to verses near the back of the Bible.

During the course of one particularly involved answer my friend leaned forward and said softly, "I wish I could be like that. I wish I had the answers to all my questions." He leaned back for a moment and then stretched forward once more. "No. I don't wish that. If I had all the answers, I wouldn't be having any fun. I'd die of boredom." He paused for a moment, then added, "I need another muffin."

He stood up and headed to the counter.

I stayed put and thought about my friend. "He's a creature of the shore," I told myself, my mind drifting to a metaphor astronomer Chet Raymo once offered. Raymo held that "knowledge is a finite island in a sea of inexhaustible mystery." Every time we add to our knowledge, we extend the shore along which we encounter mystery. The questions will never stop. We may expand our knowledge to the end of time, but the mind-stretching wonder will never cease. "Bureaucrats, technocrats, and scientific drudges keep to the high ground," Raymo wrote, "their noses fixed in ledgers and laboratory notebooks." He could have said the same about those theologians and religionists who bury mind and spirit in the too-solid clay of fixed formulas and pat answers. "We are at our human best as creatures of the shore, with one foot on the hard ground of fact and one foot in the sea of mystery."[5] It is along the shore that the truly creative work gets done. Creatures of the shore perpetually ask questions, expand the known, and open to the ever-widening mystery.

My friend returned with his muffin. The sound of the Bible study had grown softer in our minds if not in reality. We talked of our families and the days ahead. We spoke of our work. He said that he had recently thanked a woman for the privilege of letting

5. Raymo, *Skeptics and True Believers*, 46–49.

him listen to her story of an abusive childhood and how she had dealt with it. "You know what her response was? She said, 'Well, listening to my stuff couldn't be that much of a privilege!'" He laughed. "It's always a privilege." He had grown animated again, waved an arm in the air and hit his hand on the table.

The Bible study began to wind down.

"I've got to go too," he said. "I have an appointment." Then he did what always surprised me even though I knew it was coming. He stretched forth his hands, palms up. Grace in public restaurants was rare in this part of the country, and if it did happen, it invariably came exactly when it was supposed to, at the start of the meal.

"Your turn or mine?" he said.

"Yours."

He prayed slowly, pausing again and again.

> *Thank You for this food,*
> > *this time,*
> > > *this day*
> > > > *for stars*
> > > > > *and for Thomas*
> > > > > *and our families.*
>
> *Keep us open to You,*
> > *wherever we are.*
> > > *In Jesus' name we pray.*
> > > > *Amen.*

I don't know what prompted me, but that morning I asked what I had wished to for a long time. "Why do you pray in the name of Jesus?" Whatever answer he might give, I knew it would not be the customary "Because that's how we're supposed to" or "That way God will answer my prayer."

"I do it because Jesus embraces all of this," he said. "All!" He waved his hands between us, down to the gleaming nebula, then around the whole room and most extravagantly towards the pastor and cluster of Bible students heading out the door. "Nothing gets left out."

He pushed the nebula picture toward me. "Keep it," he said. "Remember, this is part of what you are. Stardust!"

I watched him go. A tall form. Stardust.

I looked at the fiery nebula he left me on the table. Somewhere, billions and billions of years ago, carbon atoms formed in the hot depths of a primitive star. After nearly incalculable eons that star exploded, scattering carbon atoms into the darkness of space where they swirled nearly forever, until they gathered into a new star. In that star's depths heavier elements took shape, and in the vastness of space and more explosions and time, the elements gathered into compounds. Across gargantuan stretches of time the compounds became a living cell, and through ages cells became a body. The bodies arced into realms of thought and love. And a mass of stardust, filled with compassion and wonder, had just walked out the door. Late in the day, that stardust would go bowling with a troubled man who desperately needed a friend.

I saw him get into his car and drive off, and as I watched I journeyed along mystery's unending shore.

4

The Storyteller

Roundabout slowness may be more accurately informative.[1]

JAMES HILLMAN

THE LAST TIME I saw the storyteller she had donned her green print dress. When nobody was around, which was nearly always, I suspect she stayed with the jeans, loose shirt, and bandanna I found her in most of the time. Today, though, I had phoned in advance for what we both knew would be our last visit before I moved away, and out came the green dress. She even had a white scarf swirled around her neck. Eighty-six years old, six feet of upright bone, muscle, and welcoming eyes, she greeted me at the door.

The first time I saw her she lay flat on her back in the hospital. Her name did not appear on any list that I had of church people to visit. I just happened upon a long wisp under a white sheet. We talked for all of three minutes. When I returned a few days later she was gone. "Fine. Went home," was all the nurse said. I didn't see her for another two years.

When I finally wound my car along a miserably rutted road through scruffy forest and arrived at her place, I'm sure it was partly

1. Hillman, *The Force of Character*, 171.

guilt that brought me. All that time I knew she was tucked back there somewhere and I hadn't done a thing about it. And partly, I am sure, curiosity tugged at me. By then I knew nearly everybody else in the region, but she and I hadn't exchanged a word since that groggy conversation two years before. After this new visit, I made the journey as often as I could. I had to hear her tell the stories.

The stories were always simple and personal. At times they were pleasant, funny on other occasions, gripping on still others. It depended on the day and her mood. Over time the content of her tales proved rich and varied. Of a truth, though, after all these years I remember almost nothing about what went on in any of them. What caught me was not the stories themselves, but how she told them.

Her narratives always had a clear A—B—C pattern to them. For instance: A) She and her husband met when she left the city for a weekend and came to the hills hoping to find some excitement; B) her parents were less than pleased when they decided to get married; C) dang, they got married anyway, were plenty happy, and, after a stretch, her parents were too. That was the whole tale. Putting it into the computer just now took almost no time. Texting would, I am sure, take still less. For the storyteller, though, the journey from A through C invariably lasted a minimum of twenty-five minutes. This was partly because she relished every detail. There would be the whole matter of her thumb-twiddling, spirit grinding boredom as a secretary in the city, and her anxious wondering of "Dear God, will I *ever* find a man who's interested in a body as tall as mine?" There would be her first glimpse of tree-covered hills when she got off the train for her weekend of exploration, and her even sharper glimpse of the young widower at the church supper "who had muscles down to his fingertips and a shy smile under his moustache." Her eyes went wide as she told such things. Wider still when "with those big hands of his he pretended, that very first weekend, to put a ring on my finger." She would pause at moments like this. Catch her breath. Scratch the dog.

"Of course when my parents heard we were getting married they were beet-red mad. This was even more embarrassing for them than when I decided to live out here on my own." At this point she was clearly shifting from movement A to movement B in her narrative. The only problem was, at crucial times like this she tended to lurch off course into matters that had absolutely nothing to do with what she'd just been talking about. "Yeah, my parents were furious." Brief pause. "Oh, did I ever tell you about Jake?" No, she hadn't.

"Well, during Prohibition old Jake kept a still back in the woods. Wasn't the best thing to do, maybe, but the poor man had to eat, and he was a good fellah, and, well to be truthful, he had a decent product." And here she plunged into a whole different narrative that had nothing to do with what she'd just gotten me interested in. She spent a fair bit of time talking about Jake, his neighborly ways, his continuing attention to the quality of his product out in the woods, and she got him all the way up to where, "Early one morning just after we got married and settled in this cabin, there was this terrible BOOM out in the woods. Well, right away we knew what it was, and at best Jake was up there absolutely flattened. Oh, and did I tell you my parents were really upset about my marriage?" And here, of course, the storyteller had shot back to what she'd hooked me on in the first place.

I found this disconcerting. It was as if I had been writing about the storyteller, her venture into a new life and her particular way of telling stories, and had even brought Jake into the picture, and then suddenly in the middle of all this wrote, "Have I told you about Anna? No? Hmmm. Well, there was a fine woman named Anna who lived up on the Saint Lawrence River where I had my first church. She and her husband lost their farm when the Saint Lawrence Seaway took it. Actually, the Seaway Authority and that awful bureaucrat Robert Moses took it. Terrible thing, but they adjusted. When I met her some years later she lived alone beside the Seaway. She loved to watch the river at sunset and had a gorgeous garden of gladiolas out back. People said Anna's gladiola garden was the best in all of New York State's North Country. Well, Anna was somewhat heavy. One day she was out back trimming her glads when she tumbled over backwards, went flat on the ground, and there was no way she could get up. And, *Oh, I meant to mention*, the storyteller did get back to talking about her parents' opposition to her marriage." With that I'd go back to writing about the storyteller, leaving Anna flattened out there beside her gladiolas, just like Jake was "at best" pancaked somewhere near his now exploded still. Never mind, either of them. Let them stay there.

"My parents wouldn't even come to the wedding" the storyteller would say, getting on with what she had been talking about to begin with. "They made up some excuse about my aunt being sick and they couldn't leave the city, but that was after they sent me two letters saying, 'Have you really thought about what you're doing?' I knew the real reason they didn't come. In the end they sent a 'Honey, we love you' note and a small check, because they were, well, decent folks and they always had a bit of a struggle figuring me out anyway. But, I tell you, they missed a good wedding!" and she was off plunging into the details—the icing on the wedding cake her husband's sister made, its sugary smoothness, the cool air that blew through their hair as they drove off for their one-night honeymoon, the frosty sunlight that pierced the wall cracks in their home those first mornings they settled into their life together, the rattle of her husband's laugh every evening as he came in from the sawmill.

She was through part B of her narrative now and well into C when all of a sudden she would veer off again. "Like I said, my parents didn't approve, but we were having a good marriage. And, Oh, Hazel! Did I tell you about Hazel?" I'd nod in the negative. "Well, Hazel was the hunting dog my husband had when we got married. BEST dog he ever had. Broke loose the night of our wedding and found us six miles away! No bother. She was a good dog" and that would be it for Hazel. No more mention. The storyteller would go right back to painting more pictures of their early marriage.

This bit with Hazel made no more sense than if I were to be sharing right here about this woman's marriage and then came out with, "Oh, Martin Buber! Did I tell you about Martin Buber? A *great* rabbi. One of the best in the past hundred years. He wrote some wonderful books. And, as I was saying, the storyteller was getting pretty well along with her narration at this point" and that would be it. I would have dropped Martin Buber as fast as she'd dropped Hazel the dog, and Hazel and Buber would be stuck out in a field somewhere wondering why they'd gotten hauled into the narrative in the first place.

Well, the storyteller would go on for just a little longer telling about those first months of their marriage, painting pictures all along the way, and then she'd make one further shift. In midsentence she'd quit what she was talking about and say "Jake! I told you about Jake back there!" She was reminding me, not asking. "My husband and I heard that awful BOOM early in the morning. We both shot out of bed and raced up through the woods. We didn't have much on, but this was no time to bother about getting into our fancies. We were worried sick about the man."

She'd scratch the dog at this point, giving me a chance to ponder the two of them charging through the woods without the benefit of their "fancies," whatever those might have been.

"We cleared the rise above his house, kept on running and what did we see but Jake himself. He was smudged but standing straight as a rod right by his old Dodge." The still was nice and upright, just behind him.

"'Dern,' he said. 'I hit the spark and there was gas in the muffler,' and he held up an inside-out, blackened piece of junk he'd yanked from under the car. He looked right at us and gave his quirky smile. Then he paused. He turned away. "

"'Thank you for checkin' on me,' he said, just like that. No frills. 'I'd invite you inside, but, uh, you might be getting a bit cold.'"

The storyteller and her husband made their way back down through the forest pretty quickly. "Holding hands, we were, and mighty relieved." She would slow down as she said this and then go back to talking about her parents. Two months after the business with Jake, they came out for a visit. They stayed in town but drove to the cabin. It was awkward at first, bound to be, but "they were good folk and still trying to understand." Jake heard they were coming. He made a point of dropping by. Having checked to make sure it was ok, he even brought his product. Her dad liked that and her mom blushed. "Then," the storyteller said, "came the best part."

"Jake said to Mom and Dad looking 'em square in they eye, 'This daughter and son-in-law of yours are something. They're too modest to go into details, even for you, but I gotta tell you a little while back they risked their lives, even their reputations, to help me when I was in a tough spot.'"

"Well, that was what parents love to hear, maybe especially when things are awkward. And," the storyteller continued, "Hazel. You remember Hazel! She did right that day too. My dad loved dogs. Before my folks left, Hazel came over and licked my dad's pants. A great big slobbery lick, right on his knee. Dad tossed his head back and laughed and laughed."

And at this point in her narrative, the storyteller would smile, her eyes looking off, signaling she was done. Sometimes she'd laugh. This day she did. Laughed out loud, head back and full.

She laughed just like Anna out there in the garden. You remember Anna? Flat on the ground at the top of New York State. "I couldn't get up. Couldn't do a thing," she told me. "So I looked up at those gladiolas and I started to laugh. It was all so beautiful, the glads, and the golden sun, the breeze, the sky, the clouds. I laughed and laughed. Must have gone on for five minutes. Then here came my son 'cause he heard something strange out in the garden. And I looked at him and I laughed, and he hauled me inside. I was still laughing when he plopped me on the couch. Just laughed and laughed. Oh God, this is such a beautiful world!"

When Anna says that about the world, I just can't help myself. I think of Martin Buber who got left out there with Hazel for a little while. As a middle-aged philosopher he groped for words to convey what he passionately knew to be true. In his finest work he declared, quite fancily, "The mighty revelations to which the great religions appeal are like in being with the quiet revelations that are to be found everywhere and at all times."[2] And also, "He that truly goes out to meet the world goes out also to God."[3] So he urged

<hr />

2. Buber, *I and Thou*, 116–117.

3. Ibid., 95.

that with our whole being we relate to all that is around us, to the laughter, the interplay of lives, and the bond between things that at first appear to have no connection at all. Cherish the details, the taste of the cake long ago, the cool wind blowing through our hair, even the dog's affectionate slaver on a waiting knee. Relate wholly. Open to what is here. Here we encounter the Holy. Here, Buber said, we meet the eternal Thou.

We meet the eternal Thou, as when at last we completely see another, tall and straight, all decked out in a green print dress and a white scarf swirled elegantly around her long neck, her dancing eyes wide open, eyes that still teach mine to see.

5

Community Organizer

JACK SAT IN THE driver's seat as we headed east out of Potsdam and across the top of New York State. Plattsburgh lay two hours away. A low October sun shone through the rear window. "Ever thought about putting a neighborhood center in the Waddington parsonage?" he asked ten miles into our journey.

"No, I can't say that I have." The two-story parsonage consisted of my office, six empty rooms, a kitchen where the two-hours-a-week secretary and I made coffee, and an upstairs bathroom. I was pastoring two churches and lived seven miles out of town in the dwelling that belonged to the country church. The Waddington parsonage was delightfully quiet—a perfect place to read, reflect, write sermons and, once in a while, hold a meeting.

"Uhhh," Jack said in response to my "No." He looked straight ahead and stayed silent for at least a minute. Jack was twenty-four years my senior. In formal terms, he was my General Presbyter. That meant that he served as my mentor, guide, pastor, and friend if I would let him. He served the same role for other ministers of our denomination across the entire region from Watertown on Lake Ontario, through the northern Adirondack Mountains, to Port Henry on Lake Champlain. I quickly learned that though he stood an inch shorter than I, he walked much faster. He could laugh uproariously, and if something was bunk he said so. A farmer told me that Jack had been an All-American hockey player at Cornell. His compact energy, feistiness, and muscled forearms left little doubt about the matter. I was also learning that Jack had a tendency to ask a single question, let it sit for a minute or so, and then follow up with a brief statement.

"Well, I was just thinking that with the Poverty Program coming out of Washington there's money due up here and it might be possible to get something going in your neck of the North Country." The Adirondacks started into view to the south of us. "Aren't they beautiful! I love this whole stretch!" Jack gestured vigorously, swerving the car as he did so. That evening he never mentioned the neighborhood center again.

Exactly one year later the toilet in the parsonage was holding up well under the strain of considerably augmented usage, primarily by the small children of mothers frequenting the Waddington Neighborhood Center. The Center had its own thrift shop where people could get dresses, pants, shirts, blouses, and kids' clothes for a dime apiece. There were also craft classes, parenting classes, plus meetings in rooms that hadn't been entered, much less sat in, for years. One day somebody used too much glue in a craft class. The middle-aged outreach worker got high and the entire parsonage had to be aired out. Gone was the quietness, the place of reflection, of blissful stillness for the crafting of sermons. Gone too, for a number of folks, were the loneliness and isolation that marked life in this beautiful but spare and economically struggling region.

If asked, Jack would have said he had absolutely nothing to do with the birth of the neighborhood center, or at least darned little. In a sense he would have been right. He never put in an appearance at a planning meeting. He never pressured me or anybody else. What came forth belonged entirely to the town of Waddington. The leadership arose from the town. The hired staff came from the town. The benefits were the town's and belonged to all the people living in the village and out on the back roads.

What Jack did, though, was keep asking questions. About four weeks after our trip to Plattsburg he was at it again. "Have you thought any more about that neighborhood center?" He didn't ask just me. He asked others who had been around a lot longer. He also pointed us to each other. "Steve, you might want to talk to George Donovan and Olive Moffett over near Canton. I hear they know something about this stuff." "Olive, you might want to talk to our new pastor in Waddington. He's a good guy, but I think he'd like some direction." When appropriate, he offered praise. "I hear you people are meeting together. Good." "I understand some of your farmers have built racks for a thrift shop. That's terrific!"

All this came early in our relationship. Jack grew visibly uncomfortable if people gave him credit for things, so I need to be quick about this next item, but I also must share it. Over the next seven years I watched him play an essential role in the establishment of summer camps for kids too poor to go to camp, free health fairs all across the northern hump of New York State, a Native American Cultural Center on an economically and emotionally depressed reservation, a program to help farmers explore the tough moral choices facing them, and more neighborhood centers.

In all of these matters, Jack stood far in the background while also being front and center. A paradox shimmered here.

As critically important as Jack was in each of these situations, everyone else was more important. And not just in Jack's eyes, but really and truly. The six-year-old who learned to swim at camp or the three-year-old whose rampant impetigo got treated at a health fair counted way ahead of anything else. They drove the whole thing. So did lonely women whose depression eased because each Wednesday through the long winter they sipped coffee and traded stories at a neighborhood center. So were church and community leaders who suddenly caught a vision of how to treat hurts that had festered on their doorstep for years. Whether they built coat racks, did the day-to-day work, or showed up for services, they made it happen. They were central.

From another vantage point, however, Jack was just as central. The term "community organizer" was just coming into fashion when he and I met in the late 1960s. I'm sure we didn't use it in our conversations until several years later. Yet long before either of us employed the term, Jack acted like the best of them. He stayed in the background. He watched, listened, and caught a vision of what might be. He asked questions, connected people, and faded back. He let others lead, encouraged them when appropriate, and coached when circumstances required. Then he faded away completely.

The paradox. The group was everything. Without the group—without all the kids needing to swim, the lonely folks on back roads, the leaders wanting to see their town better—there would have been nothing. Yet Jack too was everything. Without Jack, there would have been nothing.

I tried to figure out what made this good man tick. In part I could see it was the sheer delight of using his gifts. When he was very young it had been the thrust of a hockey stick, the quick turn on the ice, the strong shot past the goalie. He was good at it. That was joy. As he grew older the joy of giving his best continued, but he knew it had to take other shapes.

"He is the finest teacher I've ever seen," one professional educator told me. With those perfectly timed, quick-shot questions he created curiosity. With dogged patience, he would wait until just the right moment, then slide that question our way again. And however matters moved on from there, he was ready. From years of immersion in the North Country, he possessed an encyclopedic knowledge of connections. As we began to answer his questions with wonderings of our own, he knew just how to aim us and fire up our sense of what we might do. "Boy, you've asked a good question. I don't know much, but why don't you talk to Don Huddleston at the Extension Service? I bet he'd be glad to hear from you. Let me know what you find."

Jack was a linguist. Not in the ordinary sense of that word. I have no idea whether he could handle French, Spanish, or any other tongue that was current when he was in school. He had, though, an uncanny ability to move into the daily world of the people he related to, to enter their culture, to learn the language of their pains and joys, and then to speak that language with them. He did his best to nurture that gift in me though I was a halting student. "If you want to know the farmers, Steve, you've got to get out into the barns." "To understand the rural poor, Steve, you're going to have to drink a lot of dark coffee." From his lips, that wasn't a put down on the poor or the coffee. He was saying, "Get rid of your pre-conceptions. Be with them. Relate. Enter their world and receive. Listen. Then and only then can you join them in discovering what all of you can do."

Jack knew how to create tension for good purposes and how to take conflict when it came his way. If he found he was getting nowhere trying to pierce my youthful self-righteousness, he'd look me straight in the eye and come up with something like, "Your idealism is getting in the way of your better judgment." Then he'd sigh and walk away, leaving me to figure out what he just said. If he got called a Communist—which was highly inaccurate—or a male chauvinist pig—which was ridiculous and attempted only once—he might go so far as to say "Damn," but then he'd get on with what he needed to.

Jack had a gift for thinking in the plural. Like any good orga-nizer, he delighted in what groups of people could do. Among his most frequent questions was, "Do you think we might get some people over there to talk together about this?" When they did get together, he had the ability to help them discover what together, and only together, they might accomplish.

He was good at all these things—the teaching and the timing, the connections, the language, tension and conflict, building the group. I became convinced, however, that for all his gifts and his joy in using them, something simpler and deeper motivated this man. He was not philosophical. Had I asked him, "What keeps you going?" I'm not sure what he would have said, if anything. An incident that occurred late in our working relationship, though, spoke at least the beginnings of a response.

The two of us brought an honest-to-goodness, trained com-munity organizer into our region. He came for one full weekend to share organizing tactics with a large number of folks seeking to address issues of rural poverty. The group came from all over the ideological map. Sitting right next to each other were the Execu-tive of the Junior Chamber of Commerce and the guy who chaired the Welfare Rights Organization, eager young moms and quiet septuagenarian farmers, the Monseigneur Dean from the Roman Catholic Seminary and the Head of Planned Parenthood. All went well until late the second day when the organizer propounded The Iron Rule of Community Organizing: *Never do for others what they can do for themselves.*

This greatly offended some of the church people who were participating. For them it was hardhearted. It didn't fit their understanding of Jesus. And, as one Unitarian Universalist said, "This makes trash of the Golden Rule." Jack, who certainly was in favor of Jesus, had an unquestionably big heart, and did his best to practice the Golden Rule, had no problem whatsoever. He understood.

What motivated this man? That weekend I became convinced that at least in part it was a pervasive desire to see everyone else become the persons God meant them to be. The poor, the young, the old, those marginalized by race or lack of education or gender. Everyone. This was the message Jack lived consistently: whatever people's circumstance, listen to what they are saying; give them what they need to grow; then, literally for God's sake, back off; get out of their way and let them find joy in doing what they need to do. Perhaps someday I would understand even more fully what worked within him, but for the time being this was a start.

6

Seeker

Thou hast formed us for Thyself,
and our hearts are restless till they find rest in Thee.[1]

AUGUSTINE OF HIPPO

THE SEEKER APPEARS IN a host of forms. Sometimes I encounter
the seeker because I am a minister. Or I meet the seeker in a friend.
Or the seeker ambushes me as I read a favorite author or sit with a
family member I thought I knew inside and out. Every time I am
in the presence of the seeker I receive a gift. I rediscover my own
search.

*The seeker held a space for me every third Monday, 7:15 a.m.,
at Panera Bread in Kalamazoo.* He was my age, even my size and
general appearance. The first time we met I liked him instantly.
On the matter of religious belief, he had no use for "the Big Guy in
the Sky." That notwithstanding, he had come to believe in God. He
grew up with no religious instruction and could say precisely when
and where belief came. He was in early middle age, at the nadir
of a difficult siege in his life, and walking across the tarmac at an
airport. Belief hit him like the blast from a jet engine. He resisted

1. Augusine, *Basic Writings of Saing Augustine*, vol.1, p. 3.

calling himself a Christian because of the cramped attitudes he saw in a lot of people so identifying themselves. Still, every Sunday he worshiped at the church of which he had become an active member. That Jesus should be the actual son of God puzzled him. He read Reinhold Niebuhr. The Bible was a struggle. When we met we talked about all of the above plus politics, poetry, sex, and death, all of which plunged us right back into religion. He forced me to think, laugh, and give thanks. Our meetings persisted for five years and stopped only when I moved away.

Three times the seeker came to that same Panera as a brilliant young woman. An honors graduate of a fine university and a gifted writer, she found work reporting for a newspaper in the Northeast. She had never joined a church, but that didn't stop somebody at the newspaper from offering her the religion assignment and it didn't stop her from saying "Sure." She swiftly found herself in the midst of worshiping Baptist and Greek Orthodox Christians, and, of course, mellowing things out a bit, New England Congregationalists, Episcopalians, Methodists, and Quakers. After eight months she came home for a visit. Somebody suggested to both of us that we talk. When we did, her delight in what she was finding nearly overwhelmed me. I read some of her pieces. Every one of them moved me. If she had been raised from birth as a Presbyterian or, say, a Roman Catholic, or any of the groups she wrote of, would she have seen with such freshness and breadth? I have no idea. I do know that the following fall she went back to school to study theology and deepen her understanding of what she found so life-giving.

The seeker came to church one day as a truck driver. Earlier in the week, I conducted the funeral for his mother. Aside from the funeral I had never seen him in church. At some point during the service he heard the words, "I am the resurrection and the life, says the Lord." He had been invited to pray and he had been prayed for. On the way out of church the following Sunday he took my hand and said, "I just thought I'd come." His face stayed solemn. After that he rarely missed a week. When we visited in his mobile home he never asked any questions, and I felt it best not to force them.

He liked to talk about his gladiolas. The solemnity left him as he sat in the pew Sunday after Sunday. His face remained forever attentive and gradually grew bright.

The seeker came one afternoon as a couple wanting to get married. They were wary of church in any form. In the name of Christ, persons had deeply hurt their gay and lesbian friends. The man, an educator, had been harassed by fundamentalists for teaching evolution. The two wished no part in such things. Yet they did not want a secular wedding. They wanted prayers and, although they weren't quite sure why, they wanted a minister. "What we really want is God!" the woman finally blurted out, half laughing. "Does that make any sense at all?" As they explored the matter, it did. At this vital juncture in their lives, they wanted, as the man put it, "the living Presence we know is real but has been so blocked from us."

Four men stood to be received into their novitiate year in the Order of Saint Benedict. I sat in the choir with their families and friends. As the men faced the Abbot, we had a perfect view of them, three in their twenties, one middle-aged. The Abbot reminded them of the single requirement for entering the monastery at this point: they must truly be seeking God. He instructed them to live in humility with their brothers. During the year ahead they would continue to discern God's direction for their lives and whether to take their final vows. The year would be difficult. Did they truly desire to enter? With a united voice, "Yes," they did. The Abbot looked to the black-robed brothers stretching behind them. Did the brothers receive them? "Yes. Thanks be to God!" The Abbot invited the novices forward one-by -one and presented each with a robe. The four removed their suit coats. Brothers helped them don the robes. We sang a hymn. We prayed. The service was over.

The Abbot invited everyone to a reception in another building, but first, he said, it was important for the novices and the entire monastic community to have some time just to themselves. In complete silence the long line of men filed out of the sanctuary and into the adjacent abbey. The silence continued for a full minute. In the church none of us spoke a word. Suddenly a thunderous

"Hooray!!!" resounded from the abbey. Old seekers, aged seekers welcomed the new.

Four youths sat at the feet of a Buddhist monk in Bangkok's Wat Pho temple. Nearly half a century has passed, but I still see the light in their eyes. I knew nothing of the language they spoke, but I heard with complete clarity the eagerness in their questions and the warmth that pulsed through their teacher's replies. They were seekers, all.

My grandfather, at age seventy, decided it was time to write down his personal credo. For nearly a hundred pages he wrestled with the Apostle's Creed, the Nicene Creed, and the Westminster Confession. He was an attorney and a political scientist, not a theologian, but for him what a person believed was vital. For his own sake, if nothing else, he wanted to see where he stood. So he painstakingly deliberated upon God, Jesus, the Holy Spirit, the Sacraments, the Bible, preaching (some of it quite bad, he noted), prayer, the communion of saints (which puzzled him because it sounded Roman Catholic), death, and the life everlasting. Not long after completing the effort his health weakened. By the time he died at eighty-four he could barely finish a sentence. Barely, except at mealtime. Then, the plate in front of him, he would give thanks and ask the blessing. This was never automatic, never rote. The words came out one by one, in perfect order, his thin voice filled as much with yearning as with gratitude.

An artist sent me a drawing of Jesus in the mail. It was just the head, done with pencil on a 4" x 6" card. The head was small and fierce, taking up barely half the card. Jesus' hair shot out in all directions. His beard was thick, his chin and nose sharp, his forehead broad and deeply lined above massive eyebrows. His eyes locked onto whoever viewed the picture. When I received the card I stared at this intense Jesus and at first missed the words the artist had penciled heavily off to the side.

A few weeks before, I had seen samples of the artist's work on a calendar while visiting a friend in Cleveland. The colors caught my eye, and I had worked through the calendar three times when my friend asked, "Would you like to meet the man?" We drove to his apartment the next morning. He lived with two aging shih tzus above an abandoned auto shop. The dwelling was packed with oils, pastels, and watercolors. His work hung on every inch of wall available, but the bulk of it he had stored in piles. I went through the piles. The man was of Armenian background and old Armenian scenes figured in much of what he did. Women danced in wildly colored dresses, crowds pressed, couples married, men strutted down sidewalks. In some piles flowers of all sizes opened outward. He'd painted landscapes and people on the streets of San Francisco where he had lived for many years. Against one wall leaned a larger-than-life canvas of Jesus. Jesus was stark and pale except for a huge blotch of red on each hand. Next to the bleeding Jesus tottered another pile of landscapes. I started to go through it. In the middle I found myself staring at an impressionist Jesus, then a bawdy scene of fully dressed men and women naked to the waist, then a small, more literal painting of Jesus, then more landscapes.

"I don't know," the artist said, "somehow now Jesus just keeps getting in here." All this had been several weeks ago.

An hour after the drawing arrived in the mail, I looked at it for a second time. I saw once more Jesus' stark, staring face. This time, though, my eyes drifted off to the lettering on the side. There, in heavy strokes, hung the words

> ***Who do***
> ***you say***
> ***that***
> ***I am?***

7

Piercing Cry

MANY YEARS AGO A woman widowed for just three weeks called
and asked that I come by. "I have something to show you," she said.

She was in her early fifties as had been her husband. His
death was wholly expected, but that did nothing to mitigate the
loss. For two-and-a-half years he battled a disease for which there
was no cure. Both of them knew this from the start. The ravaging
of his body was as grindingly slow as it was unstoppable. I doubt I
ever had a more loved parishioner. Each week more people asked
after him than I could number. The dry wit that animated his slight
frame never flagged, nor, even near the end, did the sparkle go
from his eyes. By choice he spent his last week at a distant hospital
where others could study his condition. Late Saturday night his
wife called to say, "It's nearly over." Word spread through the community. The next morning half the people in church were unable
to speak as they walked out after worship. He died that evening.

His widow welcomed me graciously when I stopped in
response to her call. A Bible lay open on the kitchen table. "I've
found something that speaks to me," she said. She sat down and
motioned for me to do the same. Then, with mountains of wondering and grief, she read from Psalm 88:

> For my soul is full of troubles,
>   and my life draws near to Sheol.

I am counted among those who go down to the Pit;
  I am like those who have no help,
like those forsaken among the dead,
  like the slain that lie in the grave,
like those whom you remember no more,
  for they are cut off from your hand.
You have put me in the depths of the Pit,
  in the regions dark and deep.

PSALM 88:3–6

"Those words say exactly what I feel," she said as she closed the Bible.

I told her I was grateful she found something that did. It was clear she did not want to hear anything more. She simply wished to speak out loud the words she had just read.

A few days later an older resident of her community asked me if the widow had told me about the psalm she found. In response to my "Yes," the person firmly instructed me. "Those are terrible words. You've got to stop her from reading them."

No, I could not stop her. Even if I were able to, I would not attempt it. The words that came from her lips were painful to hear. I am sure they were even more wrenching to speak. But they were her words now, and as authentic for her as for the person who first uttered that psalm millennia ago. Hers now was the piercing cry. It is a cry older than any of the psalms.. Sometimes it comes loud. Sometimes it comes soft. Like the questions of the seeker, the piercing cry comes in as many forms as there are persons to utter it.

Several months after the woman lost her husband, a small boy in the same community died of leukemia. His parents were locked in an interminable divorce, so he had come to live with his grandmother and the old man she married just a few years before. The old fellow was partly deaf and spoke with an almost incomprehensible Russian accent. Occasionally people noted, "He's Jewish." The man had a few business associates who dropped by occasionally but no one he called a friend. He doted on the little one when he moved in. When the boy became sick, the man did all he could to get the best doctors. The afternoon the boy died, the man sat beside him, read out loud, and held his hand.

On the night of visitation at the funeral home the casket was open. To hide the effects of disease, the funeral director placed a baseball cap on the boy's head. When it came time for everyone to go, the old man struggled to his feet and walked toward the casket. He took the cap off the boy's head and placed it on his own. He closed his eyes and with a shrill voice called out in the Hebrew tongue no one had ever heard him speak. He split the air with ancient prayers that needed no interpretation. He gripped the side of the casket. He rocked back and forth. He shook. Then suddenly he stopped. He paused. Turning his face upward he spoke in English one last sentence and it was loudest of all: "God, you must be asleep!" Slowly he removed the cap from his head. He gently placed it back on the boy and shuffled out of the funeral parlor. I don't think anyone in the room thought of saying, "You shouldn't have said that."

The piercing cry finds multiple expressions in the Bible and for multiple reasons. It comes through grief-stricken David moaning "O my son Absalom, O Absalom, my son, my son!" It sounds through the dark cry in Lamentations:

> my soul is bereft of peace:
>> I have forgotten what happiness is;
>>
>> LAMENTATIONS 3:17

It explodes in Jesus' query hurled from the cross: "My God, my God, why have you forsaken me?" The Bible resolves none of this easily. All David can do is carry his unbearably leaden heart and press on as king. The book of Lamentations concludes with one last wavering plea for help. When Matthew and Mark report Jesus' cry of abandonment, no answer comes.

And, no, we do not want to hear any of this.

> *I am like those who have no help . . .*
> *God, you must be asleep!*
> *My God, why?!*

We wish to halt the cry, wall it off. Or if only we were able, we would snatch away whatever horrible event brought on the cry in the first place. Yet we know we cannot. Such change lies beyond our reach. And over the years I have come to see that those who dare utter the cry in its terrible fullness are ultimately the very persons who have a further word to speak. They have become my teachers. I will share here but two instances.

She came by to talk one afternoon and said, "I have done much lamenting lately." This was formal speech wholly in keeping with this formal and always thoughtful woman. Her calm demeanor fit how I knew her. As she began to talk, though, she recounted one wrenching sadness after another, all taking place in the past six months. The details were hers. It is sufficient here to say that she had been seared in her soul by persons she deeply trusted.

"And so," she said, "I turned to the psalms of lament. You know how many there are!" She read them day after day, week after week. At first she read silently to herself. As weeks passed, she increasingly read out loud. Her hurt and anger raged through the ancient words. "Some days I did not need the psalms at all. I did the yelling on my own."

For forty-five minutes she spoke of all that had happened, of pain that would not ease, anger that came in waves, lamentation that could not stop, and then, "You know, in most of the psalms of lament there comes a turning point. A hint of freshness arises, a breath of grace comes perhaps for only a moment. But there is a sense that life will begin again. Two weeks ago, for me the turning came. That is not to say things will be as good as before. It is not to say they won't. Maybe that's not even what's most important. All I can say is that a fresh way is beginning, even though I have no sense of where it will lead." She said that looking straight at me but without any lilt to her voice. She romanticized nothing.

"I wonder," she continued, "would even this hint of turning have come if I had not cried out the full depths of my pain? Is that how God comes to us in the worst? We acknowledge the horror. We face it in all its darkness. Then, in the very act of our crying out, after days and days of it, nights and nights, maybe even years, we begin to realize God is there too? Utterly spent—because that's what I was—utterly spent we start to sense the possibility of something new, even when we have no idea of what that is. Is that how God works in this? Do we absolutely need to shrill out again and again the cries that burn within us?" Her calm that afternoon spoke her answer.

The second instance came in the springtime many years ago when I served two small congregations, one in a town, one in the country. The preceding fall, a young man full of promise in the country church died in an auto accident little more than a mile from the home where he still lived with his parents. The parents were a beautiful, gentle couple, and his brother, serving in the Peace Corps, was of the same mold. Their piercing cry following the funeral was soft but deep and continued for months. Early the following spring word came that a young man from the town church had been killed in Vietnam. When the soldier's body was returned, his family wished to hold the visitation in their home. The family from the country church and the parents of the slain Marine barely knew one another. The night the front door in the home opened for visitation among the first to enter were the couple whose son had died in the fall. All four of these adults were reserved. I don't recall a word they spoke. I do remember that their embrace was holy.

8

The Hostess

I DIDN'T REALIZE THE old guys sitting in front of the counter at the insurance office weren't customers until I had stopped there four or five times. The office belonged to the hostess and her husband. At the outset, of course, I also had no idea that the woman was a hostess for anything or anybody. I did know her husband was church treasurer. He invited me to drop by the office my second day in town. When I did, he handed me my check for the next two weeks and smiled.

"Now you come back here every two weeks," his wife said as she stood beside him, arching her long form over the counter. "We'll have it for you. 'Pay them in advance!' we always say. That's how we treat our ministers. Golly. Yes!"

She strode back to the mound of paper on her desk. I glanced about. The office was clean and lacked any unnecessary frills. Metal desks faced whoever came in. A row of filing cabinets stood off to the side. The walls, painted a soft yellow, accented the daylight streaming in through the large windows that extended across the entire front. As I turned to go, three of the four old men seated in straight, armless chairs looked at me. One smiled. He and the two others had strong, miner's hands. The fourth sported a neatly trimmed mustache.

Men always sat there when I came in. Not necessarily the same ones. Personnel changes took place now and again, with the exception of the mustached fellow who never missed a day. Every time, though, the chairs were filled.

Two months passed and the first winter storm was roaring through the Black Hills when I encountered the woman from the insurance office on the town's main street, both of us hunched over against the wind. As we hurried along, I raised the matter that had been building inside me. "I'm curious. Why do you always have guys sitting in your office?"

"Oh, golly. Poor fellahs. They just need a spot where they can be with others and somebody will talk at 'em. Yes! So we give them the space, and you know me and the talking!" She took a breath and went on to something else.

At this point it is only right that I stress her use of the plural: "*we* give them the space." The man who paid me in advance every two weeks was as much a part of what went on in that office as she was. I am sure that in his mild way he encouraged what I saw. Still, she dreamed things up, planned them out, and did the talking. It was natural that I soon started to see her as the master hostess that she was.

I look back from a number of years now and make a mental list of those for whom she served the hostess role. The list includes:

- The old guys who sat in the insurance office
- Clergy of widely varied beliefs plus their spouses
- Two Norwegian bachelor farmers, her uncles, that lived outside of town
- The trash collector
- Widowers
- My dad, who also happened to be a widower
- Widows
- Her husband's entire World War II bomber squadron
- People whose names nobody else in town could pronounce

Part of what made her such an easy hostess for all sorts was her appearance. Lean and tall, she was attractive in that special way people comfortable with themselves are always attractive. She moved rapidly but in a manner that opened towards those around her. She bent over to listen carefully. Reddish blond hair framed her strong-boned face. Her blue eyes could laser scan a room in seconds, swell with laughter, or glow with a warmth that said, "I'm glad you are here."

Then there was her unique form of verbal stamina. She was neither chatty nor a gossip. In conversation, though, she could get excited. If she ran out of sentences before her enthusiasm ebbed, she would just keep things going with "Golly" or "Well" or "Yes," "Gee," "Don't you know?" or any combination of these until another sentence came along or the conversation veered in a new direction.

So here she was, our hostess. Like any good practitioner of hospitality, she varied her offerings according to the needs of those in her care –

To the old men who sat in the insurance office she gave a warm place to be and the chatter they needed.

To the clergy she gave immediate acceptance, and, over time, loving tolerance for whatever our foibles and inevitable shortcomings might be.

To her Norwegian bachelor uncle farmers she gave dignity. They did well on their own and she let them know it. On those occasions when they needed to tidy things up, or get their bookkeeping back in order, or a pep talk, or a good meal, she offered just what they were looking for. She always, though, took care of such matters in a way that let them know she was involved simply because they were, after all, her special uncles.

For the trash collector she had sticky buns. Great huge buns, dripping with sugar, piled with pecans, baked in her oven at least twice a month. "Nobody ever does anything for these people. Golly. Don't you know! And I said somebody ought to do something for them. Don't you think?"

For the widowers she provided whole meals.

For my dad, who also happened to be a widower, she provided the assurance that his son was in good hands. He spent Christmas with us our first year in the Black Hills. When she met him, the hostess blurted out what every wondering parent needs to hear. "You know, we love your son. And we really love his wife! Even more, we love those two grandchildren of yours! Golly!" My dad grinned. He had traveled a thousand miles and at that moment received the ideal Christmas gift.

For the widows she provided phone calls and listening.

For the World War II bomber squadron she pulled off what one veteran called "the best darned reunion we ever had."

To the people whose names nobody in town could pronounce . . . This was trickier. In the early 1900s immigrants from Eastern Europe settled a section of town that became known as Slovakian Alley. They were a hard-working addition to the community and possessed the ability to rattle off their names with a rapidity that nobody outside their ranks could hope to imitate. In time their descendants fanned out through the whole town, hauling with them their ample supply of consonants and superior pronunciation abilities. After decades of people mumbling these folks' names, the hostess made a Herculean effort. By the time I met her she could name up to seven Slovakian families in a single breath. "I figured those good people deserve to have at least one Norwegian get it right."

This woman possessed such a distinctive character that I was astounded when I met her twin. The possibility of a twin never occurred to me. Indeed, four days passed after I met the twin before I spotted the relationship. Gone was the first hostess's lanky form and red-blond hair. The twin stood close to the earth. Thick black hair hung halfway down her back. Her face was Native South American, African, and European Mediterranean all gathered into one. Her eyes, like those of her northern sister, captured anyone caught in their gaze, but they glowed rich brown and moved slowly. She said almost nothing. After offering a sentence or two she continued to communicate, just as warmly as her northern twin, but her communication came largely through attentive silence.

I first saw her standing in front of the cinderblock home next to the church her husband pastored in Carepa, Colombia, less than ten degrees north of the Equator. The area, which used to be jungle, was now covered with hundreds of miles of banana plantations owned by a multinational corporation. My working partner, Ruth Noel, and I arrived in a tropical downpour. The woman and her husband awaited us under the tin roof extending over the porch of their single-story home. Both smiled. Their home became our residence for the next eight days.

Pineapples in that region possess a cooling sweetness beyond any I ever dreamed existed, but consuming more than I should have on day three led to cramps on day four, and I needed to stay home. Ruth and the hostess's husband left at sunrise for another day of listening to stories from people displaced by Colombia's internal conflict. After their departure, the hostess brought me hot lemon tea and chicken soup filled with rice, carrots, and finely chopped potato. She said nothing, just smiled and motioned for me to eat.

The first two visitors appeared at 7:15 a.m. They both got soup, then talked for nearly an hour while the woman who served them smiled and, just now and again, offered a comment. I dozed off. "*¡Gracias! ¡Gracias! ¡Gracias!*" I heard as the two headed out the door.

A harried woman in her mid-forties walked in just after nine o'clock. The hostess—I was beginning to see her that way—greeted her with a smile that quickly darkened. The two went into the washing area out back where I could hear many words from the new visitor and an occasional, softer sentence from the hostess. After an hour, the two passed by the couch where I lay, the visitor still somber but looking more relaxed than when she entered. They parted at the front door.

At eleven o'clock a young woman barreled in, her arms laden with textbooks that she hurriedly spread all over the table where the family ate. On invitation, the hostess bent over, looked at the books, offered a few comments, then went to work in the kitchen while the younger one started to write a paper.

An old woman with a walking stick ambled in through the front door. For nearly an hour she traversed the one hallway extending through the house smiling every time she passed the hostess.

The young woman hurried away before the midday meal. The older one sat down to a plate piled with rice, beans, and plantain cakes. She consumed everything rapidly, then picked up her walking stick and went back to traversing the hallway. I lay down on the couch for a rest.

A knock came at the front door. The hostess opened to three women I recognized as young mothers from the church. She looked at them, nodded towards me, said something, then stepped outside to talk. I had no idea what was on their mind, but they spoke in earnest for half an hour, then left.

A little later the woman sauntering the hallway went out the door, still smiling and smiled upon.

The hostess propped open the front door for ventilation and then did something I saw only this once in the eight days I was her guest. She took off her sandals. She pulled open a weathered hammock that hung on the front porch and lay down, her bare feet slightly higher than her head. Other than the gentle movement of the hammock from side to side, she didn't budge. I couldn't see whether she had fallen asleep.

After ten minutes four giggling girls raced up the road from the elementary school which had just gotten out. For the next two hours they became her main focus, along with preparing dinner and visiting with three other people who dropped by.

At six o'clock Ruth and the hostess's husband returned. Two additional men showed up. The hostess gave them coffee. When they left, she served dinner to the three of us and her son who had just come in from school. We motioned for her to join us, but she shook her head, smiled, and stood to one side.

After dinner the woman disappeared into the small bedroom she and her husband shared with their youngest daughter. She emerged dressed in a handsome skirt and jacket. Two weeks ago their entire region had been leafleted with death threats. Had the guerillas done this? The paramilitaries? Nobody knew. She and the young mothers I had seen earlier headed to a special prayer service fifteen miles away. It was dangerous for them to be out at night, but all the more they wished to show they were not afraid. I heard her return at eleven p.m. The next morning she was up before dawn.

She arose before dawn every morning, and even earlier than usual on our last day. Ruth and I needed to be off by four a.m. As some time prior to that I heard her in the kitchen warming plantain cakes so we wouldn't go away hungry. She smiled as we went out the door, and in that moment her smile elided into another I had seen so many times at the far western end of South Dakota.

Two hostesses. Identical twins in spirit, worlds apart. From time-to-time, just for the fun of it, I like to imagine that the two of them meet. When they do so, they recognize each other instantly. The dark-haired one smiles. The tall one widens her eyes and calls out, "Well! Golly! Isn't this good! And how is it you say your name?" They don't speak the same language, but the dark-haired woman understands and offers her name. The other repeats it perfectly and follows with "Golly! Ha! This is wonderful!" The two take hands. Then a few old men join them, one with a mustache. And dark haired, sparkling-eyed children scurry to connect with what is becoming a circle, and an old woman with a walking stick saunters forth, and a trash collector with sugar on his hands, and my dad, and two Norwegian bachelor farmers, and a group of Colombian women who dare to go out to pray for peace despite threats on their lives. On and on they come. The circle grows large. Everyone joining it looks toward the twins. All start to dance now, one great circle flowing, ever expanding. And from the entire body arises an ancient, joyful song.

> *Ubi caritas et amor*
> *Deus ibi est.*

> Wherever charity and love are
> God is there.

9

Church on an Abalone Shell

He placed the object in my hands. Flat and two inches long, it came to a rounded point at one end and was no more than half-an-inch wide at its base. It glistened of pearl on one side and was light brown on the other.

"I made it out of abalone shell," he said. "Do you see the church?"

I had seen it instantly. On the pearl side of the shell, with just a few delicate strokes, he had incised a simple building with a cross above its door.

"Do you see the mountains and the clouds?" he asked. "They were already there."

I couldn't miss them. Just behind the tiny church, a roughness on the shell tumbled upward at a sharp angle. Overhead, pearl puffs, blue and white and rose, billowed all the way to the pointed top.

I knew the man speaking to me as Dave Big Bear, or Dave Johnson, or Dave Big Bear Johnson. He was comfortable with any of the names. A Potawatomi from Oklahoma, he lived in the Iroquois community of Hogansburg, NY, north of the Adirondacks in the St. Lawrence River Valley where I went to pastor two churches after I graduated from seminary. Dave and I had known each other for a few years by then, long enough for me to understand that

Dave was a devoted follower of his traditional native beliefs. Due to his beliefs, some people had no space for Dave in their lives. Over the years they called him "pagan" and "heathen." He only mentioned this twice and did so with sadness rather than any bitterness. It was evident, though, that he had been hurt. With the carefully crafted object he placed in my hands, the church carved on an abalone shell, he clearly had space for me.

"Please keep it. It's a gift" was all he said.

That was nearly forty years ago.

I look at this slender piece of shell as it lies before me. What do I see?

I see a man in early middle age, broad-shouldered. His thick black hair flows back from a wide forehead. Someone has just pointed him out to me. Hogansburg is putting on a Native Arts Fair. I have come to find a stone carver who might have something I could give to the ushers in my wedding two months off. I think stone carvers grow on trees and have no idea how fortunate I am when in response to my "Where is your stone carver?" the man I ask waves a hand and says, "Over there."

A little girl is playing next to the man when I get over to him. She is four years old he tells me. Tina. Tina's mother died just after she was born. He has stayed in Hogansburg to raise her. He gives me his name explaining, "'Bear' is my clan." He is hard at work on a carving. I watch. It cracks slightly on one side. "Ah!" he says, and breaks it to pieces. He's not angry, but he would dishonor the rock if he let the imperfection continue. He reaches into a bushel basket, hauls out another rock, and starts all over again. I tell him I would like to get carvings for the ushers in my wedding. He says all his carvings are gone. Yes, he will make the carvings I want, but this will take time. Carving is a sacred act. We reach an agreement. He stands as I start to leave. He easily tops six feet. He takes my right hand in both of his, looks me in the eye, but says nothing more. He has spoken perhaps fifty words.

I look at the piece of shell before me and remember a steaming kettle of soup. My wife and I have driven up for an impromptu

Sunday afternoon visit. He had made the soup for a friend who had too much to drink and needed to drive back to Syracuse.

"Terrible thing, drinking too much," Dave says. "I got him to stay here for a while, fed him. I did what I could." Dave passes us the soup. It is rich, smooth, all vegetables and herbs. After we've eaten, he shows us an expanding garden out back. "This is my university," he says smiling broadly. He is going deeper and deeper into native plants and healing. Tina is getting taller.

I see in my mind an exceptionally beautiful carving that appeared one afternoon on the small table in his front room where none had been before. It is a duck, wings folded along its sides, with the long neck stretching backward, eyes closed, head turned downward towards a wing. The rock is steatite, speckled green and white, from a sacred outcropping in California.

"Dave, this is beautiful," I say.

"I saw a picture in the *Geographic* of a duck that died in an oil slick," he responds. "I had to do something." The carving is for the duck.

One last image arises from this time. The sky shines bright with early summer sun. Jean and I are stopped dead at a road construction project in the Adirondack foothills south of our home. Cars stretch over a rise and out of sight. Somebody has gotten off a road grader ahead of us, unable to continue working until this larger mess gets straightened out. He stretches, then strides over to a car near him. "That's Dave!" Jean says. "He does this kind of work." He is in animated conversation, beyond anything we have ever seen. His arms go in the air. He dances. We hear an unmistakable laugh. He steps back from the car with a wave and starts down the whole line behind it. He stops at two more cars, does the same thing. How many people does this man know? He gets to us. "You're stuck too!" he calls. He waves his arms at the sky again. "Beautiful day to see you out here!" We are fine, we tell him in response to his question. And Tina? "Fine!" He heads further down the line and disappears around the bend behind us.

What do I feel as I look on this slender piece of art and friendship before me?

I feel the loss. Shortly after we saw him at the construction site, we moved to the Black Hills. We tried to call on him before we left, but didn't connect. When we made a return visit to the area three years later, we drove to his home. He no longer lived there. All anybody in town knew was that he and Tina had gone somewhere out in California. Jean began a wider search. It was the early 1980s and the best channel then was the network of Native American newspapers. He was, after all, an artist. Surely somebody would know of him. Jean wrote newspaper after newspaper. People wrote back. They were sorry. They could not help us. When the internet came along, Jean tried again. Nothing. After we moved to Michigan in the early 1990s we attended a few Potawatomi Pow Wows. On the chance that Potawatomies in the Midwest might have ties in California, we asked. People shook their heads. By the mid-1990s, we gave up the search.

What do I hear as I hold this tiny object in my hand?

The year is 2007. I hear an old man's voice on the other end of the phone line. It is soft, gentle, unmistakable. Jean and I had gone to our first Pow Wow in years. We had not even asked after Dave. We knew what the answers would be. On returning home that night, we decided to make one last search of the internet. We tried Dave Johnson, Dave Big Bear, Dave Big Bear Johnson. Nothing. Nothing. Nothing. Then, for some reason we typed in "Dave Big Bear, Native American" and up came the slender beginning of a press release: "Auberry resident Dave 'Big Bear' Johnson was recognized by President Bush and Interior Secretary Gale Norton with the . . ." and the release stopped. We called up the full release. This man, we read, had given over four thousand hours per year as resident volunteer caretaker at the San Joaquin River Gorge management area. He had educated more than ten thousand school children on the cultural history of the area. Retiring from his volunteer work with the Bureau of Land Management, he was now going to give full time to his non-profit corporation, the San Joaquin River Intertribal Heritage Educational Corporation (SJRIHEC). We finished the press release. We went to the SJRI-HEC website. A nurse named Tina served on its board.

We could not sleep that night.

The next day I telephoned the number for SJRIHEC. The corporation had two sites, the main one located deep in the San Joaquin River Gorge at a former school on the upper end of Redinger Lake. A woman's voice on the answering device there invited me to leave a message. At 5:30 that evening our phone rang.

My message had gotten mixed with another. At first Dave and I were both confused. In less than a minute, we had it straightened out. His words on the other end of the line were as they had always been. Soft, spare, to the point. I congratulated him on the intertribal focus of his work. It was so needed, I said. He instantly caught what I had included in my understanding of intertribal, and what I had left out.

"Intertribal, ah yes," he said. Then, even more slowly than usual, as if he were just musing, "Tribes. That's not just us natives, you know. The Japanese are supporting us here. They're a tribe. And you folks from Europe?" A lilt crept into his voice. "You're tribes. We're all tribes, and we all need to understand each other." He followed this with, "If you come see us, we'll have a big meal for you." Three months later we came, and he did.

What do I see as I hold this small gift in my hand? I see Dave on the shore of Redinger Lake. He is still tall. His thick gray hair flows back from his broad forehead. Across the lake slopes a meadow blanketed with wild flowers. Beyond that sharp hills knife hundreds of feet upward. On the rock slab beneath his feet cluster a dozen deep holes, worn down by native dwellers who for centuries came there to grind grain. Dave smiles into the sun.

And I see Dave just a little later, standing in front of the SJRIHEC banner outside the school's main building. He smiles even more broadly than when he stood on the shore of the lake. His immense arms stretch wide, even wider than they did that day the sun shone and all those cars were stopped in the Adirondacks and he greeted friends. His arms embrace Tina and his twenty-two-year-old granddaughter on one side and his sixteen-year-old grandson on the other.

I see the two dozen certificates of appreciation lining the walls of his office. He is modest and would have none of them on view except it helps to have them there for some of the visitors. Right next to letters signed by the President of the United States and the Secretary of the Interior hangs the simple slab from a tree better than two feet in diameter. Cut into it are the signatures of twenty penitentiary inmates. They thank Dave for the care he showed while they worked under his supervision.

My mind rests on the note that arrived in the mail after we returned home. In dark ink and Dave's still steady hand it reads, "May the Great Spirit bless you."

What lies in the palm of my hand? What is this piece of tapered shell that cradles a church and mountains and billowing clouds? It is the gift from a man whose love knows no bounds. To hold it is to feel something as solid, and as piercing, as an arrowhead.

10

Quiet One

FOR SIX YEARS I watched the quiet one. Something drew me each time I saw her over town or glimpsed her at the back of the congregation on Sundays. I could not then say how she first aroused my curiosity or why she held my attention so steadily throughout that span of time. Over the years since, though, certain recurring images and the interplay between them have helped me understand.

A girl balanced on a railroad track as if walking a tightrope, her arms stretched wide to the side. Her right hand clasped a burlap bag with three pieces of coal in the bottom. With her left hand she pointed to a black lump glistening beside the tracks ten feet ahead.

"Up there!" she called to her littler sister.

The girl on the tracks was nine, small for her age. Her face was long and thin. She smiled slightly as she called, "Up there!" Her sister, three years younger, dashed forward, grabbed the coal, stood on tip-toe, dropped the lump into the burlap sack, and then heard, "Good!" from her older sibling.

The older girl knew it was getting late. The time between school's end and darkness had grown short. Before long they would have to go home. Some days the trains going to and from the mine dropped lots of coal. Some days they didn't. Yesterday was good, except her arms ached from carrying home such a heavy sack. Today was a disappointment. Six lumps. Snow would fall in less than a month. As soon as her little sister dropped the coal in the bag, they headed farther up the tracks. She hoped they would find at least four more lumps before they had to turn around.

"We were outcasts," she said when nearly eighty years old. "My father was a union man. A lot of people had nothing to do with us. Even those that liked what he was up to kept their distance, except when they came by for the late night meetings in our kitchen and Mother served hot coffee and the men talked low. We never had money for enough coal to get us through the winter, so my sister and I went out on the tracks." She said this softly, one hand resting against the side of her head. A slight smile of recollection sent creases all over her face.

The young girl balancing on the track strained her eyes. More coal? She sensed what lay ahead. Whether she and her sister arrived home with a full sack or with one nearly empty, as it looked like would happen today, she would hear, "Good work. You did your best." She knew that would be true. After dinner she would sit at the kitchen table and read by the lantern until bedtime.

As she moved forward on the rail she tottered, then advanced more steadily. In the next half hour she called out "Up there!" only twice. She finally looked at the sky and said, "It's time to go home."

In the twilight she and her sister wordlessly made their way back along the tracks. They passed houses where the children didn't have to go out looking for coal. When she entered her home, she placed the limp sack just inside the door. Her father's beard scratched and felt warm as he hugged her.

A slender old woman pulls a cart behind her. She has on the blue, calf-length coat she wears every fall, winter, and spring. In winter she adds a brown scarf, red mittens, and a furry black cap. "They keep me toasty," she said one day. Today, though, is October 2. Her coat is unbuttoned. She lifts her face to the breeze. Her straight hair, still mostly brown, blows out behind her.

In the cart she has three days' worth of groceries. That is always what she gets on Wednesday and as much as she can haul up the long hill. She has not stopped once. Her pace is neither quick nor labored.

A man walks towards her from the opposite direction. He is ten paces away. If the man greets her, she will smile and nod. If he passes by without acknowledging her, she will still nod and smile just slightly.

I watch all this from the insurance office across the street. One of the old guys passing the morning there has just told a joke and two others are laughing. The female co-owner has someone on the phone and rattles through the stack of papers on her desk saying, "Let's see! Let's see!" A second phone rings. The woman's husband picks up, listens, then yells, "*Hi, Bud!*" and keeps yelling because Bud is deaf. The fellow who told the joke decides to try another, only this time he talks louder to make himself heard over the conversation with Bud.

The scene across the street has just concluded in perfect silence. The man advancing down the hill said nothing. The old woman nodded, smiled, and kept on.

In another ten steps she stands at the entrance to her apartment, a second-story walk-up above an abandoned garage where the city used to keep two snowplows. She has lived there for decades.

She hefts the food cart over the one step and disappears into the enclosed entry. The inside stairway is steep, and getting three days of food up to the apartment will take two trips. The apartment, I know, is as simple and adequate as the woman's blue coat. A couch and a few comfortable chairs in the main room. A kitchen. A bedroom. Some books in the bedroom and the main room. No television. "Why would I ever need one of those?"

As I walk away from the insurance office, I glance across the street and see a flash of blue through the entry window. She has come back for the rest of the groceries. Saturday she will head down the hill again. I have no idea what she will do between now and then.

The photograph measures 5 by 8 inches and probably sat on somebody's desk. In it she is neither the young girl nor the old woman. Her clothing dates the picture to the 1940s. A bookcase lined with legal volumes rises behind her. She stands and looks downward.

A portly man wearing a three-piece suit sits in front of her at a large wooden desk. He signs the letter that she has put before him and upon which she has fixed her gaze. The photo portrays exactly what it was intended to. The man has just completed something important with proper secretarial support. The stout fellow is, for that era, the region's most prominent attorney.

"Most prominent and the most flamboyant!" says the man showing me this photo from his collection of past notables. He does not elaborate on "flamboyant." He continues to look at the woman behind the attorney.

"She was four times smarter than he was. She stayed in the background and out of his personal life, but everyone knew she did the work and kept him as organized as he was ever going to get."

The most pervasive image I hold is of her smile. It was forever spontaneous and always subtle. Even in those situations where I grew to expect it, as when I would see her pass strangers on the street, the slight lifting of her lips and genuine brightening of her eyes came as a surprise.

Shortly after I became pastor of the church where she worshiped, she and another member made an anonymous gift to repair the sanctuary. Three weeks later the other person decided to go public and wanted a large brass plaque put up announcing the gift. I asked the quiet one what she thought. That was the first time I saw her smile. "Oh, my heavens, we don't need that." She talked to the other person. The plaque never went up.

In time I learned that this woman who wore the same blue coat year after year was extremely generous with financial resources most people never knew she had. She kept her name as far from the gifts as possible, but after a few years I knew what she was up to. As we visited one day in her apartment, I mentioned her generosity and how helpful she was to so many. "But don't you see?" she said, "This is how it's meant to be for us." The smile came. She went quiet for a little while, then changed the subject.

A major storm struck her community the last November our family lived there. Fifty inches of snow fell in less than a day. Drifts reached twenty feet. For a week, half the town lost electricity, including the section where she lived. Two days after the storm, a plow cut a single lane past her place. Late that afternoon two teenagers and I hacked our way to the apartment doorway. We hurried up the stairs. Everything was stone cold. We could see our breath. Our faces stung even when we stood right next to her door. We knocked. The door opened.

"Come in." She scurried back under the quilt she had wrapped around her while sitting in her usual chair. Then, just after getting snug she sat up straight. "Tea?" The smile broke loose. "You're cold. Would you like some tea?" She stood before she finished asking the question for a second time.

Somewhere along the line she had laid in a lifetime supply of Sterno cans plus a small metal oven on which she had been heating tea, oatmeal, and bread.

All of us sipped the tea and ate the bread. She got warm under the quilt. A kitchen timer suddenly rang for five seconds and quit. "That's how I'm telling time," she said. She gave the timer a twist. "Good for another hour!" She made a hash mark on a small pad of paper. "Let's see," she said half to herself, "the sun comes up around 7. Ten marks. Must be about five o'clock."

She thanked us as we headed out the door, told us she had enough food and not to worry. The corners of her mouth lifted one last time. Her eyes shone through the clouds created by our breath. The door shut. She went back into the silence.

Years later I heard of a woman who in old age whittled her prayers down to just one: "Thank you, Lord, I am content." Whatever came along, she offered the prayer and meant it.

That easily could have been the prayer of the quiet one. I still, though, cannot say what formed her into the whole, contented person I knew. Was it, simple as it sounds, the love she received as a child? Was it some early lesson she gleaned while coping with her family's isolation? Was it the joy she took in smiling at strangers or in living sparely and giving abundantly? Did the person she aged into have anything to do with the satisfaction of knowing she had used her mind well, despite having to work years for a man who owed more to her abilities than he did to his own? Or did her hidden uses of solitude in some way nurture contentedness? I suppose all of this had a part in who she was. All I now know for sure, though, is what drew me to her from the very start. Inside this quiet soul, something deep was going on.

11

"How beautiful you are, my love . . ."

PEOPLE WAITING FOR THE train to arrive weren't that crowded in the waiting room, so there was no need for the two of them to press together the way they were doing. The station was warm, so he did not have to hold her hand that firmly. Or was she more holding his? This was difficult to figure. The clasped hands regularly disappeared in the narrow crack between their bodies. Then, still clasped, the hands would shoot around behind her back or his.

And there was what she did with her free hand. She lifted it, this ancient, bone-thin comb of a hand, and raked it slowly across his chest. For how many decades had that been going on?

They didn't need to laugh out loud the way they did. Everybody else talked quietly, or read, or stared into space.

Why did the eyes of these two keep lighting up? The train had not arrived. Much less were passengers streaming in from the platform. Their eyes, however, never glanced at the chalkboard where the station agent occasionally posted new arrival times.

I did not speak to them.

I never came upon the two again.

Nearly fifty years have passed. After all these years I still see the tug of war between their hands, the closeness of their bodies, the smiles that would not quit. Now and again, as I think on them, other thoughts enter my mind.

In the second century CE, Gnosticism sundered matter and spirit. It held that matter was evil, created by an inferior God. The high God of Jesus had nothing to do with matter. Salvation came through mystical knowledge by which people entered into communion with the world of the spirit. Gnosticism denied Jesus' humanity and rejected the reality of his death. Both were an illusion. Gnosticism turned its back on the Incarnation. It considered our fleshy substance to be of no value whatsoever.

The early church declared Gnosticism a heresy.

Of all the books in the Bible, the Song of Solomon most revels in the flesh. The Song's primary singers are two lovers. They ardently pour forth love for one another. They delight in one another's bodies. Their words are all breast and loin, thigh and mouth. The opening leaves no doubt about where the book is headed.

> Let him kiss me with the kisses of his mouth!
>
> Song 1:2

From here nothing grows slack. The images stream from another cultural world, but their surging joy needs no translation

> My beloved is to me a bag of myrrh
> > that lies between my breasts.
> My beloved is to me a cluster of henna blossoms
> > in the vineyards of En-gedi.
> Ah, you are beautiful, my love;
> > ah, you are beautiful;
> > your eyes are doves.
>
> Song 1:13–15

At the close of the sixteenth century a youthful John Donne came up with this in his Elegy XX, "To His Mistress Going to Bed":

> Licence my roving hands, and let them goe
> Behind, before, above, between, below.
> O, my America, my new found lande[1] . . .

That is memorable. But what are those words when compared to the lingering body-part-by-body-part eye-scanning sweep of the Song? The man pours forth—

> How beautiful you are, my love, how very beautiful!
> Your eyes are doves behind your veil.
> Your hair is like a flock of goats . . .
> Your teeth . . .
> Your lips
> Your neck . . .
> Your two breasts . . .

Nothing gets left out. All is joy.

> You are altogether beautiful, my love;
> There is no flaw in you

> SONG 4:1–7

The woman responds as fully –

> My beloved is all radiant and ruddy, . . .
> His head is the finest gold; . . .
> His eyes . . .
> His cheeks . . .
> His lips . . .
> His arms . . .
> His body . . .
> His legs . . .

Everything is gazed upon. All is exhilaration.

> His speech is most sweet,
> And he is altogether desirable.
> This is my beloved and this is my friend . . .

> SONG 5:10–16

1. Donne in Gardner, *The Metaphysical Poets*, 54.

To the devout Jew, this was not titillating text. By early in the Common Era the entire Song was regarded as sacred.

Shortly before his death in the year 2000, comedian, composer, author, and first host of the Tonight Show, Steve Allen addressed a gathering at the General Assembly of the Presbyterian Church (U.S.A.). He talked about what he saw happening to comedy. He spoke of "the greats," George Burns and Gracie Allen, Jack Benny, Jackie Gleason, and the Meadows sisters. Their comedy never degraded others. Humor lay in the cleverness of language and the amusements of the situation.

And comedy now? What was it becoming? So much of comedy today, Allen said, depends on making others look foolish or—and this upset him most—giving a five-year-old kid some four-letter word to speak and then having everybody think it's funny. What on earth, Allen wondered, does this do for the child? What is it doing to our society?

Two months later, at a motel in the Midwest, a television got switched on briefly. A situation comedy played in mid-course. The male lead, a widowed dad living with his five-year-old son, had just brought home a date. In thirty seconds of viewing it became patently clear that the woman wasn't worthy of the leading guy. She did, however, have a good figure and wore a tight dress. After meeting the child, she sauntered off camera.

The little boy gaped in her direction. Then he swiveled to his dad. In a high, squeaky voice he shrilled, "Golly, Dad! Do you see those tits?!"

Adult laughter, pre-recorded and stored for just such a time as this, exploded.

For the first time all evening, the college chaplain stretched a hand towards the Bible lying on the table next to him, a Revised Standard Version bearing more hints of his treasured King James than its successors. "There's one last thing I'd share with you," he said. He started to turn pages in the middle of the Bible, looking for the passage he had in mind.

During the preceding week, in the college snack bar and on the streets, whenever he felt it appropriate, he mentioned that on Thursday he would host a discussion of sex at his house. Ten of us turned out. For all the bravado that cut loose in the dorms whenever the subject came up, he did nearly all the talking that night.

He shared with us no warnings. No photos of disease. No tales of unwanted pregnancies. We'd gotten all that in our youth groups and the week of junior high biology when the boys went to one room and the girls to another. He offered no insights from "how-to" manuals and no "hey, guys, you'll want to try this one some time!" Nor did he spread before us a romantic vision of the sexual freedoms that were just then breaking forth.

Instead of anything we were used to, he talked about how astonishingly different two human beings can be. He spoke of the deep joy that grows when two such different persons come together sexually. He talked of continuous discovery, of work together that would not stop, and of unexpected freedoms that flourish in the context of long-term, committed love. It was for us to fill in the specifics of how all this would happen. We would, he knew, do that with our imaginations. He encouraged that. More importantly, we would fill in the specifics with our lives as they unfolded through the years.

He continued to look for the passage he wanted, then suddenly said, "Ah, here. I've found it." He adjusted the Bible's distance to his sight. He read slowly. "From Proverbs,

> Three things are too wonderful for me;
> > four I do not understand:
> the way of an eagle in the sky,
> > the way of a serpent on a rock

the way of a ship on the high seas,
and the way of a man with a maiden."

Prov 30:18–19 (RSV)

Spring had just claimed the mountains around us. Trees flushed green. Flowers pressed from the earth. Our college was all male and the nearest women's school was 60 miles away. The chaplain knew us well. With a slight wink, or the twitch of an eyebrow as he read "the way of a man with a maiden," he could have stirred an instant response. Banter would have rolled. All he did, though, was place the Bible back on the table and thank us for coming.

We walked out into the warm night. We moved slowly and said little. We had been in a cathedral. We had stood on the high rim of a canyon and felt the beckoning touch of its breezes on our skin.

Reverence permeates the closing portion of the Song of Songs. Sings one lover near the end:

Set me as a seal upon your heart,
as a seal upon your arm;
for love is strong as death,
passion fierce as the grave.
Its flashes are flashes of fire,
a raging flame.
Many waters cannot quench love,
neither can the floods drown it.
If one offered for love
all the wealth of one's house,
it would be utterly scorned.

Song :6–7

No wealth can touch this treasure. Passion flames forth fiery, unquenchable. So, "set me as seal upon your heart." The seal will bind the two lovers in closeness always.

The aged couple disappeared quickly after passengers piled off the train. The smiles they had for one another flashed outward to the family they had come to greet. They all hugged. Then they were gone. The last I saw, the two still held hands. The man walked with a hefty limp. Their heads tilted close to one another.

12

The Maestro

"MAESTRO" WAS THE LAST word on earth he would have used to describe himself. If someone had ever called out, "Maestro, how do you want the sopranos to sing that line?" he would have smiled politely and given a professional answer. As for the rest of Kalamazoo's Bach Chorus, at least forty-five out of the seventy of us would have craned our necks to see who asked the question *that* way. No doubt the questioner intended respect, but "maestro" can suggest pomp. Pomp did not fit the thoughtful, unassuming man who stood in front of us week after week, lifting his arms but never a baton. "Jim" worked better.

Jim dealt with the same issues that confront the directors of most large choirs. The Bach Chorus had ten voices any director would die for. They belonged to superb musicians with perfect pitch, ringing tones, and magnificent control. Added to them were the rest of us: sixty lovers of music, decent singers, and all but a few willing to practice between rehearsals the way we were supposed to. Some among us were gifted with astounding volume. Others, often softer, were more polished when it came to singing the right notes. Several of us, myself included, could suddenly issue the warbling vibratos that in our youth we vowed would never come out of our lips. Jim's capacity to blend all this into a seamless sound had nothing to do with grandiosity and absolutely everything to do with his humor, patience, and dogged persistence.

Still, as I watched Jim over the years, "maestro" suited him perfectly and in a manner that left all hints of pomp in the dust. Never was this more evident than in one matter that came up the spring he prepared us for a May offering of Mozart's *Requiem*.

By early March, he had introduced us to the entire work. He now focused on our blend, the finer points of Latin pronunciation, and the nuanced handling of difficult passages. Near the end of a two-and-a-half-hour rehearsal, he asked us to stand and sing the final movement just one more time. We were tired but offered as well as we could:

> *Requiem aeternam dona eis, Domine,*
> *et lux perpetua luceat eis,*
> *Cum santis tuis in aeternam,*
> *Quia pius es.*
>
> Grant the dead eternal rest, O Lord,
> and may perpetual light shine on them,
> with Your saints forever
> because You are compassionate.

Jim held us through the final note long and strong. He gave the cutoff and invited us to sit down.

All recordings of the *Requiem*, he noted, ended in precisely the manner we had just followed. All except one. "Leonard Bernstein held that last note forever, letting it get softer and softer until, after an age, it was gone."

Jim once asked a class of college students why they thought Bernstein did that. "A young woman," he noted, "gave the answer. She wasn't a music major. I think her field was English. She said," and he just stopped here for a moment and looked around at the whole chorus. "She said Bernstein was trying to show the movement from time to eternity."

He stretched out his arms and asked us to stand up.

"Sing the final phrase with everything you have."

In response to his beckoning gestures we sang as powerfully as we had all night. With shaking hands he urged us to grow louder still. We caught breaths as we needed to. The sound turned into a massive wall.

He dropped his hands for the cutoff.

We stopped. The wall roared on through the auditorium.

"Once more," Jim said in the silence that followed. "Just that last chord." He started us at exactly the volume with which we had ended. All sense of *You are compassionate* moved into that one sound. Jim held his hands high above his head. The chord poured forth, and forth yet more as he drew us on. Then, with just the slightest motion, his fingers folded in and his hands started down.

Slowly, the chorus got softer.

Jim's hands came to the level of his shoulders, then descended just a little lower. Ever so slowly he drew his closed palms close to his chest. The sound became as soft as any we had sung all night.

Jim now did something we had never seen before. At an almost imperceptible rate he curled his head forward, then his shoulders, then his whole body. Eventually his hands were above his head, but only because all of him was moving downward in the slowest of free-falls. The sound grew gossamer, still present but more felt than heard.

"You could define art, then, as a passionate desire for accuracy," wrote English philosopher T. E. Hulme.[1] We had met Jim's passion for accuracy more times than we could number. We met it when he drilled us on certain passages again and again, and at dress rehearsals yet again. We saw it in his hands. He never mentioned why he had abandoned the baton. After three rehearsals, though, any newcomer understood. With the slightest forward movement of both palms, or the cupping of just one finger and a thumb, his hands conveyed musical subtleties in a manner beyond the capacity of even the most deftly wielded pointed stick. And there were his eyes that sometimes closed and his whole body that swayed as he ushered us through long flowing phrases. His desire

1. Hulme, *Speculations*, 162.

for accuracy now, though, extended towards something infinitely larger than tonal precision, dynamics, and musical phrasing.

He was nearly at the floor. The seventy voice sound lay beneath a whisper.

Scientist Banesh Hoffman has likened our human journey to that of persons on a crowded escalator "carried relentlessly forward till our particular floor arrives and we step off into a place where there is no time."[2] Ancient Persians made a distinction between *srvan daregho-chvadhata,* time with a fixed duration, and *zrvan akarana,* the realm of eternity. The God of the Jews fashioned all that lives in time and yet is *m-olam ad-olam,* from everlasting to everlasting, transcending all of time. Platonic philosophers, Jungian psychologists, modern physicists, Hindu and Sufi mystics employ vastly different vocabularies. Ancient and modern, they have sprung from highly varied soils of human experience. Yet all reach toward a realm that lies beyond time. None captures it fully, but for each that realm is utterly real.

All sound had ceased. The chorus stood still. Jim had formed a ball on the floor. The maestro. No one in the chorus budged.

He got up slowly. "I don't know how I'll ask you to sing the ending when we give the concert. I really don't. You will just have to watch me."

He sent us home.

The weeks following contained the unexpected. Less than a month later Jim told the chorus that his father in the South was gravely ill. The next week several of the most talented singers led the rehearsal while Jim attended the funeral and spent time with his family. Shortly afterward my father-in-law, a dear and vital presence in my life for many years, died following a lengthy illness. When I returned, rehearsals had moved into the customary pre-concert intensity. Jim never again mentioned the Bernstein ending of the *Requiem.* He held the last chord as the strongest of the entire work, even at the dress rehearsal.

The concert fell on a Saturday evening. The Tuesday before, a chorus member quietly told the rest of us that as we approached

2. Hoffman Introduction to Abbot, *Flatland,* iv.

Saturday we would also be approaching what would have been the eightieth birthday for Jim's father.

Mozart's *Requiem* begins with mournful, limping tones from the strings. The chorus enters with the basses, then layer upon layer rises through the sopranos, all singing, "Grant them eternal rest, O Lord." A lone soprano arcs high above, "You, O God are to be praised," and the chorus pleads "Hear my prayer . . . Grant them eternal rest O Lord, and let perpetual light shine upon them."

Jim led us through this opening movement of the fifty-minute work. He drew us on in the *Kyrie*, "Lord have mercy," and the extended *Sequenz* with its mounting sense of judgment and prayers of love for the departed. He brought us into the more hopeful, driving rhythms of the *Offertorium* and *Sanctus*, through the solemn peace of the *Benedictus* and the pleading *Agnus Dei*.

We had come to the final movement. The solo soprano began high and lyrical: "Light eternal grant them, Lord." The chorus joined, interwove, called hopefully on God's compassion.

We reached the last note. We watched the man standing before us, his arms raised.

Professional music critics are an unpredictable lot. Sometimes the reviewer does not appear to have read the program notes or even been in the same concert hall. At their best, though, such figures articulate what the performers and audience have experienced but may lack words to express. As matters worked out, Jim took the traditional ending for the *Requiem*. At his direction, the chorus and orchestra held the final chord with thundering strength. After this, total silence pervaded the hall. In an unusual comment the next morning, the critic for the Kalamazoo Gazette noted that at the very end of the concert "Turner brought his musical army to everlasting light and eternal rest."[3] He then alluded to a soft clapping that at first just rippled here and there, and then grew into a nearly forever standing ovation.

3. Wedel, "Bach Festival Artists," Arts & Entertainment Section, Kalamazoo Gazette.

13

Blithering Advocate

MABEL WAS DEAD SET against the pizza parlor that a couple of entrepreneurs wanted to build next to Saint Joseph's Nursing Home. So were a lot of other residents of the home, but Mabel was particularly articulate on the matter. In the first place, the canyon running between Deadwood and Lead was already much too crowded. Sure, the vacant lot next to Saint Joseph's was the last one available, but nobody needed another spot where cars could pull out and get smashed into. And good heavens, the poor folks at Saint Joseph's got little enough sleep as it was. The last thing they wanted was pick-ups heading in and out at night, screeching their tires and flashing lights into the residents' rooms when they were getting ready for bed. Furthermore, this wasn't going to be your ordinary Pizza Hut. They were going for a liquor license and that wouldn't improve matters for anybody except, perhaps, for the people who sold the liquor. And then there was the simple fact that residents occasionally wandered out the front door of Saint Joseph's when they weren't supposed to. What if one of them was quietly laboring across the pizza parlor's parking lot when a car zipped in?

Mabel was not a person to fool with. Her posture alone carried authority. When she was younger, she must have stood six feet tall. By her mid-eighties she had gone down to five feet, ten inches but still held herself as erect as she possibly could. She moved steadily, planting her walker with a firm thump at every two steps. Theologically, she knew where she stood. "I'm a Baptist," she said the first time we met. On those occasions when I led Sunday afternoon service at the home, she invariably asked that we sing "The Old Rugged Cross."

Mabel also had a deft touch. Saint Joseph's possessed a good staff, but a couple of them used the Sunday afternoon service as a depository for people who didn't want to be there. One such Sunday I started to read the Twenty-Third Psalm. I went at it somewhat loud and still, I hoped, expressively.

"The Lord is my shepherd, I shall not want."

"Sonny, for Pete's sake" yelled a woman right in front of me, "preach to yourself!" The woman was strapped in a chair and had been dropped off without a lot of say in the matter. Mabel sat next to her and, with squinted eyes, encouraged me to press on.

I did and got partway through the final verse, "Surely goodness and mercy shall follow me all the days of my life . . ."

"I said, *damn it*, preach to yourself!" the woman howled.

I suppose one definition of hell is having to listen to the Twenty-Third Psalm when you're not in the mood. Mabel reached over and gently took the woman's hand. She looked at me as if to say, "We'll all get through this." It was rough, but we did.

So Mabel, unflappable, deft, staunch, set out to halt the pizza parlor. Or more positively put, and as she herself would have expressed it, she was just trying to make her neck of Lead-Deadwood a little better, or at least keep it from going downhill. In the afternoons she planted herself in the lobby and buttonholed anybody who walked in Saint Joseph's door. She talked to the staff. She chugged up and down the hallways working on the residents. Objectively, she had a good case. The last thing the canyon needed was more crowding. Another spot to get liquor didn't make sense. Even if it did, placing the proposed parlor next to a nursing home was a lousy idea. Still, overcoming a couple of entrepreneurs would take, as she considered the matter, some darned good organizing and a massive show of force.

Mabel caught me one day just as I entered the home to visit some parishioners. "There's going to be a meeting next Wednesday. The sponsors of the parlor will be here. They know there's trouble. They want to tell us how good it's going to be. You come! It will be in the activity room. Eleven a.m."

I checked my calendar and said, "I'll be there."

"People all over this nursing home are saying that," she shot back. "Just 'cause they say something doesn't mean they'll do it. You be there!"

I vowed I would and went on to my visits. Mabel hung back in the lobby poised to grab any more clergy who happened through the door.

The morning of the meeting I arrived five minutes early. The crowd was sparse. I could see a few members of the Saint Joseph's staff, two residents aside from Mabel, four other clergy, the head of the local Chamber of Commerce, and three people from the Town Council. Two men in dark suits sat behind a table up front. One was portly, about thirty years old, with thinning blond hair that he had neatly combed forward. He alternately beamed at the tiny crowd in front of him and looked down to adjust his suit coat over his stomach. The other, rail thin and a little older, sported a moustache and a thick mat of black hair plastered tight to his skull. He moved papers back, forth, and then back again on the table.

Then there was Mabel. She sat near the back of the room surrounded by empty chairs. Her gaze shifted regularly from the chairs where nobody sat, to the door where no more people entered, to the beaming blond fellow up front working with his suit coat. Her large hands draped limply over the front bar on her walker. I had seen Mabel a couple of times when she was tired, but I had never seen her crestfallen.

One more minister straggled in.

It was 11:10.

"Well, it's so good to see all of you here!" the portly fellow piped up. "I guess it's time we begin." He flashed an exceptionally enthusiastic smile. He told us how glad he and his friend were to be coming to our area. His friend nodded. He said how excited they were about the good location. The dark-haired fellow nodded again. This place was easy to get to, he said, and with Saint Joseph's Home right next door they'd have such nice neighbors! His hands never stopped working as he talked. They went up and down, out front, sideways. He told us in great detail about the menu they'd offer. His friend held up a large poster. I confess I like pizza, but until this extended part of the presentation I had absolutely no idea how many pizza combinations are possible. He then told us about the building they would construct. His friend held up a sketch. By now the speaker was working up a sweat. With considerable zest he told us exactly how the building would be put together, what materials they would use, the number of people they would hire for doing the work. His friend held up several more charts. Finally, he said that the most important thing was they wanted to work well with the community. "So," he paused and gave his widest smile yet, "do you have any questions or concerns?"

At first nobody said a word. We had been there for a good while and were getting hungry. Then somebody from the Town Council ventured "just a quick question" about the timetable for the construction. The answer came swiftly. Building would start as soon as the coming winter was over. One of the clergy politely inquired whether, in light of the two men's experience, they might have anything to say about nighttime noise or other issues that could affect the nursing home residents. "Oh," beamed the man in charge, "there'll be no troubles. None at all. We'll all be a happy family here!"

He then looked around quickly for any more questions. Mabel's hand started to rise.

The fellow stood on tiptoe and pointed. "Yes, ma'am, *waaaay* back there all by yourself!"

"There's one more thing you need to hear," Mabel said. She spoke slowly. All color had drained from her face. Buttonholing pastors and talking things up with the residents day after day had been all right. It had even been fun. Taking on the powers that be when the army of backers you counted on hadn't shown up was an entirely different matter. Mabel's voice was tremulous in a way I'd never heard it before.

A recorded message over the intercom announced lunch in the dining hall, but whatever Mabel's condition, she was gaining momentum and would not be stopped. "There's . . . one . . . more . . . thing you need (cough) to hear," she said, repeating herself and doing it very slowly.

"Some of us in here are old." She wrenched herself into a standing position. "Sometimes we forget what we've just said. We forget what we've just done."

She paused and adjusted her hands on the walker, took a breath.

"We love this place! The fine care. The games!" She looked at the staff. "The worship." She nodded one-by-one to each of the clergy. She hesitated, then nodded at each one of us again. "Some of us in here are old. We forget what we've just said. We forget what we've just done. Did I just say that? We sometimes get confused. Confused! And when we get confused"—she was speaking very slowly now and staring hard at the two men—"when we get? Confused!"—I couldn't tell whether she was acting or just at the end of a marathon campaign she saw collapsing all around her and had decided to go down with it—"when we get confused (cough) some of us wander out the door and leave (long pause) St. Joseph's behind. And wouldn't it (*cough*) be just awful if one of us got out at night, or maybe a whole bunch of us got out one night with our walkers and wheelchairs and canes and ambled over to your pizza parlor to take an innocent look, or maybe even buy one of your lovely pizzas, and a pick-up zipped in and we got smashed to smithereens right in your parking lot? Wouldn't that be *awful*?"

Mabel looked as startled as the two men who had just received her message.

In my mind's eye I can see a woman from the Town Council mouth a silent "Yes! Mabel, you said it just right!" This, though, is a fabrication of time. It didn't happen. At least not outwardly. I do know that for a moment Mabel looked like she wanted to say more. She fumbled, seemed to be reaching for words, then thought better of it and plopped down in her seat.

"Well, ma'am, that was lovely," said the lead fellow. "We'll always want to hear comments from our public." His smile was still in place, though it had obviously been there for an awfully long time.

At that point a second and quite firm announcement for lunch sounded over the intercom. Everyone, including Mabel, left the room as fast as they could.

I didn't see Mabel for another four weeks. When my turn came to lead Sunday worship, she was right there in the same spot as always. Her color was good and her energy fully restored. She requested "The Old Rugged Cross" and during prayer time asked if we could please give thanks for what by then all of us had known for a couple of weeks. For some reason or other, there would not be a pizza parlor going up on the lot next to Saint Joseph's Home.

14

Umbrella Moment

MY WIFE AND I were attending a conference in Oregon when, in July of 2006, Israel bombed Beirut. Of course Israel was responding to acts of violence against its own people, and those acts came in response to other acts, and those other acts had arisen because of still other acts. We learned of the situation early on Tuesday morning as we headed out of our dorm room for breakfast. The Conference Coordinator stood in the hallway with her laptop trying to get on wireless that "doesn't work worth a hoot in my room. Did you hear Israel bombed Beirut last night?"

The conference ended Friday and we flew home to Michigan. By then missiles were crashing into northern Israel. One of Jean's closest friends married an Israeli after graduation from college. For nearly 30 years they had lived on a kibbutz in the northern part of the country. For several years Jean's friend met regularly with Muslim, Jewish, and Christian women, all of them seeking to bridge the divides of centuries and end what they regarded as senseless slaughter.

The day after we returned, Jean e-mailed her friend to ask how she was doing and tell her of our concern. Less than an hour later our phone rang. When Jean picked up, I could hear her friend's "Thank you!" even though I was seated at the far side of the kitchen. A missile had landed in a field a hundred yards from their dwelling. Other than that, they were okay. Their conversation quickly turned to grief. Grief over violence returning yet again. Grief over fear burned further into the minds of children. Grief at intransigence on both sides of the never-ending conflict.

Late in the afternoon a friend called to tell us that a local group planned to hold an hour-long peace vigil the next day along the main route through downtown Kalamazoo. After this, every-one would walk to the city's central green for a few speeches. "Yes," we told the caller, we would be there.

When we arrived, we took our place at the far eastern edge of a line that already included two hundred people. Shortly after-ward a family of six came along. The woman carried an infant. She wore a black hajib and a loose gray robe that fell straight from her shoulders to the ground. She smiled gently at both of us as she took her place in the line and guided the next-to-youngest child, a boy, with her free hand. Her husband held hands with their two older children, both boys. The eldest wore a bright red t-shirt with white letters across the front: "Muslim Youth for World Peace."

"They're all boys," the woman said smiling at Jean and antici-pating a question about the infant.

"How old are they?"

"Eleven years old, seven, three, and eight months."

"You're busy."

The woman smiled again.

The two shared both words and silence. When they talked, they spoke of their hopes for children, of Jean's teaching, of the four boys in the family, and of family members living at great distance. Jean spoke of her friend in Israel and of her meetings with women of other faiths. The woman listened and nodded. The father and I played some with the two older children. For most of the hour we simply stood. His smile was the same as his wife's, giving and receiving at once.

"Now it's time to go to the park," a monotone voice called through a bullhorn.

The entire line of people started toward the gathering place two blocks away. For the first time I was grateful we had brought the umbrella along, an oversized model we purchased as Band Parents a few years before. There had been reports of major storms over Wisconsin early in the morning, but the sky was just a hazy blue when the vigil began. Suddenly clouds started to build. As we headed for the park, wind blew. People broke into tight clusters. The sky went gray-green. The wind got worse. The clusters picked up speed.

In the park, people jammed together in front of the band shell. Still no rain. The sound system quit and left the first speaker in pantomime. The sky went black. Then the system kicked in and blasted the speaker's words into unintelligibility. A technician shut the whole thing down, fiddled with it, got it going again, and the speaker had just started back in when the rain hit. Huge drops of rain, then sheets, then whole Niagaras.

I looked about for the family we'd stood with. All I could spot were arms going up over heads, people huddling, families scurrying to get under the few trees in the park. Some raced toward the bandstand. Then, ten feet away, I spotted a black hajib on a body bent over smaller forms beneath it. "Here, here, take this." I thrust out the umbrella. The face in the hajib looked up. A hand grasped the umbrella and shoved it skyward. The family pressed together. Children were lifted in arms. All six figures formed a single, lumpy knot under the protective canopy.

Seconds later I heard, "You! *You*, come here!"

An arm stretched far out into the rain, hurriedly motioning to Jean and me. The two of us pressed in. We now had eight people under one umbrella. There was no more than an inch or two between our adult faces. The kid's heads pressed into our bellies and thighs.

At that moment, as the rains hit their peak, the young face looking out from the hajib nodded as much as space would permit, first to Jean and then to me. What she offered came without affectation. "Isn't this really what it is all about?" she asked. Again without any affectation, she smiled.

I would like to say that woman's "Isn't this really what it is all about?" and her smile represented the final movement of the day. This would make a good ending. After all, what was that moment under the umbrella but a sign that in the midst of hatred's most terrible storms persons can nurture something warm and life giving? That, however, was not the ending.

The rain continued another three minutes, then ceased as quickly as it had begun. The speaker resumed her talk. After less than a minute, though, other voices arose from the crowd. Harsh voices. Angry voices. Voices of violence. "Jews are not human!" "Death to the killers!!" Nobody knew where these people came from. A man got on stage and seized the microphone. One storm had ended, but another worse than the first engulfed us.

I looked about for the Muslim family. I could not see them. They had already done what people all around us were doing. It was what Jean and I knew we needed to do as well. We could not wrench back what had been snatched away. By staying we would only give credence to what we could not possibly endorse. We left.

That good moment under the umbrella was fleeting. To imply anything else would amount to nothing more than sentimental indulgence. Toxic, hate-filled forces held sway even at this gathering for peace. These were the same forces that for centuries, sometimes through persons claiming to be Christians, or claiming to be Jews, or claiming to be Muslims, have denied the faith they say they represent. In the midst of violence, that woman's smile and her words came as a tender but fragile gift, as fragile as the good efforts for peace of our Israeli-American friend and her Jewish, Muslim, and Christian sisters in northern Israel.

And yet I think it distorts nothing to consider that, on a far deeper level, the very fragility of that woman's smile and the weakness of her words make her offering all the more on track. We have paid too little attention to the matter, but the record shows that even in the natural world it has happened more times than can be numbered: the fragile, the pathetically weak becomes the future's dominance or its prize. Eons ago, on a continent whose outlines we would barely recognize, a giant form rumbled across the late

Mesozoic plain while a furry creature with four tiny paws and the capacity to nurse its young scurried out of its way. Would that lumbering form even have noticed the miniscule bit of fur? And eons before that, something slender glided past a cluster of trilobites as they inched their way along the bottom of a shallow Paleozoic sea they had dominated for millions of years. That slender form had no outer shell for protection. It sported what appeared to be a useless, barely covered string of nerves running down its back. It is preposterous to imply the trilobite wondered at the fish. It would be the crudest form of anthropomorphism to ask, "Did the thunder lizard think, 'What is this tiny bundle scurrying about my feet?'" The principle of surprise, though, has been present throughout the long unfolding. The pathetically weak, that which is laughably insignificant, heralds the breakthrough into whole fresh realms of being.

This happens on all levels.

"Can anything good come out of Nazareth?" "Of course not!"

"Did you hear? Prince Gautama left the palace to sit under a tree. What a fool!"

Change has always come this way.

Mathematician and theologian Beatrice Bruteau notes that when society practices *agape*, which she defines as the promotion of the wellbeing of one another, "the cosmos will be performing, on this very complexly organized level of itself, a divine act."[1]

The young woman looked out from her hajib. Her sharing was swiftly crushed, but in that moment under the umbrella she dared point to something new. After years I still see her smile and hear her words amid the roaring of storms. "Isn't this really what it is all about?

---

1. Bruteau, *God's Ecstasy*, 163.

15

The Communicant

By their gifts of grace, the sacraments write their law of love in our hearts. They bring the most sacred and the most pressing obligation. The more we are ready to follow their urging, the more open we are to receive all their riches. Then they will go on and on making us messengers and witnesses of the love of Christ.[1]

BERNARD HARING, C.SS.R.

A YELLOWED PAGE IN the journal I kept many years ago carries the following notation:

> It is Holy Week. B. came to Communion on Maundy Thursday. Frail. In pain. He bowed in prayer through much of the service, but once when I looked at him he raised his head and smiled at F. He was radiant. He left quietly when worship ended. Many were moved.

The letters shake. I was obviously in a rush, too pressed to note the matter neatly, but I felt what I had seen too important to let slide into oblivion.

---

1. Haring, *A Sacramental Spirituality*, 281.

Bob was just shy of seventy years old when he came to communion that night, his frame much altered from the man I had met three years before. He had shown up on our doorstep the day after we moved into the parsonage, toolbox in hand and ready to work on a problem that the plumber had not quite resolved before our arrival. He stood tall, had a wide dome of a forehead, strong cheekbones, and an easy smile. He looked first to the kids, then to Jean and me with eyes that said, "Welcome!" before he spoke a word. Our house had a small alcove inside the front door that he filled when he stepped in. I moved backward into the front room.

"Ha!" he said, "you've noticed I'm big! Here, look at this," and he turned around, modeling the back-side of his pants for the whole family. He pointed to a large triangle of light tan fabric extending several inches downward from his waist. "Flo, my wife, calls that a Retirement Wedge. I gained twenty pounds after retiring from the mine last year. Flo told me *You can sew that one on by yourself!* I did a pretty good job, don't you think?"

Bob went to work with his toolbox. In short order, much to everybody's satisfaction, we had a functioning toilet.

"That's what the Church Trustees are for," he said as he headed out the door. "If you need help again, give me a call." He bounded down the steps, hefted himself into his white pickup and carefully edged onto the narrow street that descended steeply past our new home.

Later that afternoon the pickup appeared in front of the wood frame house up the hill and across the street from us. The oldest couple in the congregation had lived there for decades. The man was dying at a V.A. hospital in Minneapolis hundreds of miles to the east. Their one child had died many years before. I glanced at the pick-up several times and finally saw Bob and Flo come out of the home together. She was as petite as he was large. They held hands all the way to the pickup.

Every day for the next several weeks the truck appeared across the street. Sometimes Bob and Flo came together. Sometimes just Bob showed up, particularly after the November snowstorms got going in earnest. When he visited alone he walked back to the pickup more slowly than when Flo was along. Often he stood by the door of the vehicle for a time, took in the mountain air and looked over the rolling expanse of whiteness and ponderosa pine that descended for miles until it disappeared into the mist hanging over the plains.

The night the old man died Bob called to tell me. I went across the street to see the widow. Bob and Flo sat on either side of her. She thanked me for coming, but "Please," she said, "I hope you won't be offended. This is terribly hard and I just want to be alone." She hesitated for a moment, then continued. "Well, no, I really want to be with Bob and Flo. I hope you understand and don't mind."

It snowed fiercely the next two days. Each morning, the white pick-up parked out front. The mounds of shoveled snow got as high as Bob's head.

At some point around this time I heard Bob say "I've got cancer. Had it for a few years." He told me one day when he was fixing a faucet at the church. He added, "I'm in remission. Things are going well." That was the end of it. He just wanted me to know.

During this time I also got a fuller picture of the man. Bob himself provided the first part of it one afternoon as he, Flo, and I sat in their kitchen. "I couldn't believe it when I got hired at the mine. Nine hundred of us were camped in town looking for jobs. The Depression was at its worst. The farms were ruined. I'd come up from Nebraska. Other fellows had hitchhiked, ridden the rails, even walked from all over the Dakotas, Wyoming, and Montana. Nine hundred! The mine bosses kept our names on a list. Every morning one of them would climb up on a platform. We'd all gather. He'd tell us if there were any hirings. Most days all we heard was, "No hires." Then one morning the man up there called out, 'One job.' He yelled my name. I had to ask the fellow next to me to make sure I'd heard right."

The rest of the picture came from others. Young and powerful, Bob went to work underground. The bosses noted not only his strength and persistence in chasing Black Hills gold ever deeper into the earth. They also saw his easy manner with others, even men twice his age. Before long, he was supervising a small crew. When he

retired forty years later, miners were extracting ore from better than
a mile down and Bob had major responsibilities for large numbers
of them as they descended at all hours of the day and night. He also
served several terms as president of the City Council. He lacked the
instincts of a political fighter, but in a community of differing and
often clashing views, he was a bridge-builder and forward looking.
The respect of others, rather than aggressive campaigning or wheel-
ing and dealing, placed him in office.

I also learned that back in the days of his greatest physical
strength, he spotted Flo. She was quick-witted, athletic, half his
size, and worked as a milliner in Deadwood, just down the mountain from the mine. He wooed her and won. "They raised as neat a
bunch of kids as you're ever going to see," an Elder in the congregation told me a couple of months after we'd arrived.

Soon after the funeral for the man across the street, an incident occurred that further formed my image of Bob. He stopped
by my office one morning to tell me a young woman from the
community had been cut out of a relative's will. She needed the
small inheritance that was coming to her, but the only other member of the family, an older man who hadn't been to the community
for twenty years, recently paid a visit and turned the benefactor
against her. The young woman learned that she had no inheritance
less than twenty-four hours before she was to sing at the benefactor's funeral. She went ahead and sang anyway, with the person
who had wronged her sitting in the front pew. I was there. She sang
beautifully. "She's keeping it to herself, but she's hurt," Bob said.
"It's not the money that has her upset. It's the rejection by someone
she loved." The night before the funeral she had sought Bob out.
She just needed someone to talk to. She spoke of the situation to
no one else. "I thought you ought to know," Bob said. "Maybe you
could keep her in your prayers. She's injured."

Winter pounded along, then ebbed into April when the
afternoon sun sent torrents of melted snow down the streets. By
mid-May aspens glistened green all the way from Sturgis up Boul-
der Canyon into Deadwood and then still higher into Lead where
mineshafts gleamed silver against a turquoise sky. In the midst of

this shimmering freshness, a parishioner approached me on Main Street one morning with, "Did you hear? Bob's cancer is back."

"Saying 'it's back,' puts the matter a bit strongly," Bob said when he, Flo, and I visited that afternoon. He wasn't in denial, nor was Flo. "Oh, I've got cancer, that's for sure." He was, though, looking at comparisons. What he had before was prostate cancer. Now it had cropped up in his bladder. "There's a lot the doctors can do, and we're going to work at it." From Flo: "You bet we are."

For two years they worked at it. Sometimes everything went well. Sometimes "More needs to be done." After a full year everything looked good. Then, early in the summer, Bob let me know "Some more cells have cropped up, but the doctor will go after them." Heading into the fall, all was going well again. Throughout this time, Bob and Flo gave his health all the attention it needed, but weren't obsessed with it. Mostly they visited the kids and grandkids, saw folks in the community, helped out at church, and answered more times than anybody could number the question, "How are things going for you?"

Another spring had arrived when Bob called one morning to ask if I could go with him to Rapid City that afternoon for a doctor's appointment. Flo had a meeting she needed to attend. The doctor might give him a bit of a test. If that was so, he would need a driver on the way back.

Bob looked wan when he picked me up, but over the last two years I had seen him that way various times, and his speech was as vigorous as ever. The hour ride went quickly. The doctor was on time. Neither of us knew exactly how long the appointment would take. Bob came out after less than ten minutes, smiled at me, and motioned for us to head to the truck. He took the driver's seat, put the engine in gear, and we headed home.

"Well, the doctor tells me there's still a little bit more they can do for me," he said as he pulled onto Interstate 90. He knew "a little" really meant "not much." Then Bob started to talk about living with cancer. He talked about his fears when it all began. He talked about a longtime friend with prostate cancer who offered him counsel the night before his first surgery. He talked about

coping with uncertainty, and the importance of family communication, and love, and how "for Flo and me these have been just the
best years ever."

Bob was a careful driver, but as we went along he kept turning and looking directly at me for just a second or two. After this
he would face ahead, say more, then turn again, catch me in the
eye for an instant, then focus back on the road. Halfway home it
dawned on me he wasn't trying to fill the time or engage in some
kind of personal review of how he had handled things. He had, at
this point, become my older brother. He wanted to share all the
insights he could in case somewhere down the line I found myself
making the same journey he was on.

When we reached town, I asked if he wanted me to be with
him when he gave the news to Flo. He thanked me, but said she
would be all right. He would be okay too, and probably it would be
better if the first conversation was just between the two of them.

The "little bit more" the doctor said they could try did nothing. By fall, Bob's weight loss was obvious. One day in January as
he, Flo, and I were visiting, Bob said, "I know what's happening to
me. It won't be long." He asked if I might suggest some scripture
passages for him to turn to. "I'm not afraid. God has been good
to me all these years, and I know God will be good to me now. I
would, though, just like to read a little each day." I gave him the
passages and inwardly prayed they'd help.

The cancer advanced without letup. By early spring, going
anywhere became too much. Flo appeared each Sunday in church.
She answered the inevitable slew of questions. She carried greet-
ings home to Bob. The three of us met for briefer and briefer peri-
ods, always in their kitchen. As Holy Week approached, I offered
to bring him communion at home. Bob responded by asking about
the time of the Maundy Thursday service and said that "if possible"
he wanted to receive communion that night with the community
he had so long been a part of.

Bob had accented the "if" in his answer, so when he appeared
at the back of the sanctuary that night, I was as surprised as everyone else in the congregation. The outside elevator was broken, so

he had climbed eight cement steps to reach the entry. He moved down the aisle quickly, supported by Flo on one side, and grasping pews with his free hand. His face breathed pain. He sat immediately when he got to his usual place and bent over, hands clasped.

Bob remained bowed through the beginning words of the service, the first hymn, the scripture readings, and the sermon. He lifted his head at the words, "This is my body which is broken for you." He received the bread and the wine sitting in the pew, and then bowed again.

It was at some point near the end of the service that he raised his head once more and turned to Flo. I felt compelled to preserve this detail when I wrote so hastily in my journal, and even "radiant" does not convey his expression at that moment. I doubt any word could. Benedictine scholar Kevin Seasoltz has written of Holy Communion, "We come into the presence of the Lord like a beggar with an empty bowl trusting that the Lord will fill it."[2] With what had Bob been filled? That night he did what he had done for years. Over and over again, he had let himself be filled with the love that he then took back to Flo and his family, that he took to his co-workers and to all who needed someone who would listen to them or who would hold their hand in grief or offer a word that years later might be of aid. Now, though, he had received the sacrament at the farthest point on his movement through time. Had he, a beggar with his empty bowl, opened more fully than ever? Had this good man stretched across all barriers and in this moment known the Eternal Presence?

It did not matter that none of us got to ask such questions. We really didn't need to. Bob received a gift that night and we saw it. With his unforgettable expression, he spoke of something that lay beyond all words. After the service, leaning on Flo and catching at the pews, he made his way up the aisle and quickly headed for home.

2. Seasoltz, "One House, Many Dwellings," 419.

16

Singer

MADGE WINKED AT HER husband and then at her youngest child as she strutted on stage. Never mind that the stage was actually the front of the church sanctuary in the narrow space between the pulpit and the first pew. Never mind that the sanctuary at absolute capacity, which it always was for the Annual Amateur Night, held only eighty people. Madge shot her arms over her head like she stood in front of ten thousand. She wore no rhinestones to go with the country songs she was about to belt out. Rhinestones in any quantity cost too much. She had, though, donned her absolute best, which meant she wore the brown pantsuit that made it to church every Sunday and had added a large bracelet to her right arm. The bracelet shimmered as she waved at the crowd. She paused, grinned over the whole bunch, then nodded to her grown daughter who was tucked in at the piano. The daughter played four bars. Madge opened her mouth and started to sing.

I don't remember a word of the two songs that followed.

What I remember is my shock at the size of Madge's voice. Set Madge outside the church and that voice would have cut straight to the river a mile away. She thundered her way through the first song. When the second song turned sweet for a few bars, she got soft as a sparrow. I recall too what she did with her body. She was, as her husband liked to say, "kind of compact." When she started to sing she stood stock still, but as the rhythm began to pulse she worked her arms back and forth in perfect time with the beat. Then her shoulders got into the act. Occasionally, and unpredictably, she'd point at some startled onlooker and give a big wink. Near the end of the second song she opened her arms wide over her head, her short fingers pointing to the ends of the earth. When she took a bow by nodding her head just slightly forward, it felt like she hugged everyone in the room.

The crowd went wild.

They got that way every year. Madge always came last on Amateur Night. That was a good decision for everybody's sake. Before my first year there was done, I learned she sang in front of people only one other time as the calendar rolled around. On Christmas Eve she offered "Silent Night." The same grown daughter accompanied. Madge didn't move an inch when she sang this. There was nothing but the muted sound of the piano, a pure mezzo voice from somewhere in the shadows, and the birth of Christ. Every year the congregation fell quiet.

On Amateur Night, however, all hubbub broke loose once Madge was done. After the cheering died down, everybody squished down the stairway to the fellowship room. Pies came out and tubs of ice cream. Little kids who had played the fiddle got hugged by grandparents. Old guys shuffled off to a corner where they wouldn't get bumped into while reminiscing. Teens yelled at other teens across the room.

My first year, I made the rounds struggling to remember names and chatting with as many people as I could. At length I came upon a petite woman, barely visible in the crowd. She identified herself as Madge's mother. She had curly white hair, stood two inches shorter than her daughter, and weighed a good fifty pounds less. I made the obvious comment about how well Madge had done and how gifted she was.

"Ah, that Madge!" she gestured with her hand that wasn't holding the pie. "If things had been different, she could have gone to Nashville." She paused and kept her eyes fixed on her daughter.

At that point somebody pushed between us and the conversation ended.

In another fifteen minutes people started to clear out. The cleanup crew went to work. Women scrubbed plates. Men stomped garbage, stuffed it in the trash bin, and sealed the bin extra tight so the raccoons couldn't get at it. I joined a teen as she swept the floor and set things up for Sunday School.

A warm breeze was blowing when I got back to the car. No moon. Just a ton of stars. I started up the dirt road. No traffic. There never was, but at night the brown belt unwinding in front of me was even more barren than usual. And wholly quiet. I found myself thinking of Madge and smiling.

I heard her mother's comment, "If things had been different she could have gone to Nashville." Of course independent of whatever prevented her from going to Nashville in the first place, what would have been different was simple. She could have made it. Or at least she would have had a solid try. I had sung in a number of groups by then and knew that voices like Madge's hardly ever come along. And there was the infectious glint in her eye and her ability to climb inside every head that turned her way. Instead of having eighty people in the palm of her hand she really could have taken on ten thousand. That would have been different.

And if she had made it her clothing would be different. Not the brown pantsuit she wore Sunday after Sunday, but something glistening like her smile. Her dwelling too, would be different. Not the trailer that got a small room cobbled on every time she and her husband had another kid. Not that but some white-columned mansion. And if things had been different she wouldn't have to get up at five o'clock every morning to cook hash browns and fried eggs at the Hot Spot Diner out on the main road. Then there was the fellow she had married nearly a quarter of a century before. He was a nice guy from the little I had seen at this point, but he was at least twenty years her senior. If she had gone to Nashville surely there would have been somebody else.

I came out on the main road. My thoughts shifted. "If only things had been different." What things did that mean? Obviously

Madge's mother had something in mind, but in the next eight years I never heard what it was, and it was not my business to pry. If something wicked or juicy lay in the past a couple of gossips would have happily informed me within two months of my arrival, but I had not heard a word. I did know both Madge and her mother lived on the edge of poverty. Life had probably always been that way for both of them. Perhaps that was caught up in her mother's "If only things had been different," but even this I never knew for sure.

I pulled the car into the alley behind our house. It was getting late. Thoughts of the evening faded from my mind, except that I heard Madge singing as I turned in for the night.

Over the succeeding years I saw Madge in other settings. Primary among these was her kitchen. Never did I see Madge in the kitchen just by herself. One kid or another was nearly always there, ranging from the eldest son, thirty, who lived away but popped in every Friday, to the piano playing daughter, a paralegal who lived on her own but dropped by at least twice a week, then the twin sons, sometimes living at home, sometimes away, depending on where the jobs were, and finally the early teenage daughter who liked to hang around the kitchen to hear the adults talk. Plus there was Madge's sister who came for two months every year just to get away from things back home, plus two cousins who showed up for coffee every afternoon at 2 p.m. when Madge got home from work. I could count on seeing any combination of these.

Whatever crew happened to be present, Madge handled them with sparkling eyes and rapid-fire words, just like she was on stage. "Homework done? Well, if you haven't done your math, get to it. Now!" "How's your back? I don't care if it costs money, if your back still hurts, see the doctor! And for Pete's sake stop lifting stuff you shouldn't." "Boss any nicer this week? Uh. I'm sorry."

Madge took on projects of varied duration. Occasionally during the summers strangers moved to town. Within a week Madge was on their doorstep with a mess of beans. A week later she would be back with a bushel of zucchini, six recipes for fixing them so they didn't taste like zucchini, and ample time for a chat. By the end of the summer these people would be eating at the Hot Spot and showing up in church.

"Did you know Madge raised me?" a young mother said one day as we visited in her front room. "Not that I lived there. But for four years, every day after school, I went to her home. Half the time I stayed for supper. That was where I found sanity. I wouldn't have made it through high school if it hadn't been for her. If it wasn't for Madge, I wouldn't have waited for the right guy to marry and I wouldn't have gotten our child baptized and be trying to be the kind of mom I am."

As for Madge's husband, I initially regarded him as another of her projects, but on that I was off base. At their twenty-fifth anniversary celebration they jostled like kids when they cut the cake in the church fellowship room. His grin nearly sliced his weathered face in two. Madge's eyes glowed even brighter than when she bowed on Amateur Night. Nobody could tell which of them initiated the kiss, but it set off a thundering cheer. Then the two decided it was time to quit kissing and eat cake. They waved at everybody else to do the same.

"That Madge, if things had been different, she could have gone to Nashville." I'm sure of it. As the years passed, though, my picture of what would have changed if she had gone and become a star became more accurate than the list I drew up on my drive home the first night I heard her sing. If she had gone to Nashville no young mother would have said, "You know, Madge raised me." Outsiders would have been welcomed, I am sure, but an essential personality would have been missing. Crowds in that church would have cheered others on Amateur Night, but I doubt they ever would have cheered so loudly. They would have fallen silent for another's singing on Christmas Eve, but would they have done so with such palpable reverence?

If Madge had gone to Nashville, that trailer's kitchen would have offered space to others, but would there have been so many? Would grown kids have come back week after week, year after year because that home was still one of the best places on earth? Would a couple of lonely cousins have shown up every afternoon at two?

And would that craggy-faced guy with a mustache have grinned quite so fiercely on his twenty-fifth anniversary, or would Madge have kissed anybody else so long in front of a howling crowd?

It makes no sense to romanticize any of this. All of it took place in poverty's shadow. Madge herself never spouted pieties about life, not even good ones. Sayings like "Bloom where you are planted" or "I say to God, 'You do the worrying and I'll do the work!'" hadn't made it into her vocabulary. Some Sundays she came into church, sat up straight, and beamed all over the place. On others she bent over in the pew as much as her form would allow and stayed that way until the first hymn started. That was about all she ever said about life and faith and what got her through, but it was more than enough.

Sometimes though, I still like to imagine that I finally mustered the courage to ask the question that arose the first night I heard her sing. In the scene that develops, I always ask it after we have known each other for some years. Realizing I'll never catch her alone in her kitchen, I go to the Hot Spot after the first shift of diners has cleared out and nobody else is there. "Two eggs, scrambled, and bacon," I say. "And Madge, just between us, uhh," I'm doing my best to sound offhand and relaxed here, "if there is something you could change about your life, maybe just one thing about, say, your circumstances, what would that be?"

She arches an eyebrow to let me know I just asked a waste-of-time question. She thrusts a finger between our noses. "You! You're supposed to watch your cholesterol!" She glances around the empty diner pretending others are there, then hunches close to my ear and whispers, "I've got eggbeaters. I'll fix 'em up pretty." In four minutes she's back. The eggbeaters are fluffy and covered with freshly chopped green peppers. Two slices of dry wheat toast cling to the side of the plate. She points to the toast. "There's your bacon!" She fires a few well-aimed questions. How is my cardio diet going? Am I getting enough sleep? How are my wife and the kids? She talks about two of her grown children and a new neighbor she wants to meet. I finish the meal. I go out from Madge, and I feel good the rest of the day.

17

Evening Dance

Man speaks with many tongues, tongues of language, of art, of action; but
the spirit is one, the response to the *Thou* which appears and addresses him
out of the mystery.[1]

MARTIN BUBER

ON A WARM SPRING evening, nearly 300 people sat in a concert
hall on the campus of Kalamazoo College to hear a recital by cellist
Anthony Elliott. The second number on the program was listed as:

Cello Suite No. 1 in G Major   J. S. Bach

Dancer: Cristie Lynn Jenuwine

Prelude

Allemande

Courante

Sarabande

Minuets 1 and 2

Guige

---

1. Buber, *I and Thou*, 39.

Elliott had moved his chair to the left of center stage after his opening concerto. African-American, tuxedo clad, he sat with his long profile to the audience. He stared across the stage looking neither expectant nor bored. He simply waited. Christie Lynne Jenuwine entered barefoot from the right. Blond hair hung to her shoulders. Her ruffled skirt and loose blouse shimmered white.

Elliott raised his bow gently, then struck the strings hard. The first notes of the Prelude came strong and quick, with rapid runs up and down the middle register and an occasional high note held for a moment, then dropped as all sound plunged back into the lower tones again. Occasionally Elliott swayed an inch or two. His eyes had closed. On high the notes his shoulders raised almost imperceptibly, waited, then settled as the lower notes raced on.

Jenuwine stood still, her eyes wide and set on Elliott. Halfway through the piece she leaned ever so slightly in his direction. For a moment she raised a toe, then settled it down on the stage again. Near the end she squiggled several toes at once.

The Prelude ended abruptly. Neither figure moved.

The Allemande began slowly. Elliott dipped into the darkest notes of the cello's range. Languorous rhythmic patterns emerged from upward inching phrases. Step by step the beats came. High trills broke loose, held together by the steady, resonant return to the lowest, richest notes. Jenuwine stood absolutely still through the first half of this longest movement in the Suite. Responding to no note in particular she finally lifted several toes again, held them upward for a few seconds, then let them fall on the floor. She leaned further into the sound that poured on her, her face remaining fixed on Elliott. Tentatively she stepped forward. She made small motions with her legs in a tiny part of the stage. On the final notes of the Allemande, she opened her arms and raised her hands until they were almost shoulder high.

The Courante took off at a run. The triple time notes shot forth almost faster than Elliott could play them. His left hand spidered all over the fingerboard trying to keep up. His right arm jerked, twitched, yanked the bow back and forth. Jenuwine, keeping time with nothing at all, dropped her arms. She continued to stare at Elliott, then her feet, her muscled legs, her whole arching body began to move. In an instant she no longer stood in the tight space that had held her. Her motions became random, wider and wider, never fully one with the beat but just as rapid. She spun, ran, leapt. She had been seized. Elliott passed completely from her gaze. Her look penetrated everywhere.

And the music stopped. Jenuwine halted.

The opening of the Sarabande flowed. From the first note Christie Lynn Jenuwine moved in perfect time, catching every nuance in the music, each hesitation in rhythm. She perched on every rise in tone. She glided over the stage, stretching ever more outward. Elliott, long and straight, swayed side to side, eyes closed. Bach led the pair. He had them both.

Violinist Arnold Steinhardt dreamed one night that Johann Sebastian Bach came and danced with him. Bach wore no wig and had on 20th century clothing, but Steinhardt knew him right away. He wanted to play his violin for the master, but Bach waved the instrument aside. He tried to ask Bach questions, but the composer grabbed his arms and began to dance, occasionally saying, "Bend, spring, land" and humming to himself.[2] As a student years before, Steinhardt became absorbed in Bach. "Perhaps Bach was a stand-in for the rabbi or priest I never had—a prophet whose music moved me deeply but seemed nonetheless beyond my grasp."[3]

Grasped by the master whose capacity to move lay beyond the ken of masters all over, Elliott and Jenuwine completed the Sarabande in perfect unison. They passed together through the romantic pulsing of Minuets 1 and 2. Elliott was as he had been from the beginning, the source of every sound and at one with everything that came forth. Jenuine moved utterly free, infused with all that surrounded her. Her arms went high, steps light, bends at the waist generous. All was dignity and grace. Then, with no pause, the last piece exploded. The Guige. The joyful dance. Lightening quick. Shortest of all movements. Jenuwine sprang. She leapt. She kicked.

2. Steinhart, *Violin Dreams*, 212–213.
3. Ibid., 129.

And then she slowed.

Elliott continued in perfect tempo, chasing spiraling notes upward. His eyes remained closed, as they had throughout the Suite. He inclined his head just slightly over the entire instrument.

Jenuwine stopped in the place where she had begun. Her feet splayed on the floor. She gazed towards the tuxedoed man with the cello. On the final phrase of the Guige she leaned forward and raised both hands to her mouth. At the last note she opened them outward and blew a kiss to the man, into the sound, into the Thou that had enlivened them both.

18

The Astounded

SOMETIME BETWEEN TWO AND four in the morning the day T's
wife died of cancer, he saw an aura around her. For seven years
they had battled the disease together. In the final weeks their children returned from various parts of the country to help her die at
home. Auras weren't on anybody's mind. Seeing to the details of
the situation was more than enough.

At the start of the woman's last full night, her two daughters
administered the usual medicine. Movement of any kind had become extremely difficult for her. So had speech. For a week she had
said almost nothing.

After receiving the medicine, she slowly ventured, "It's
possible."

Acting on intuition, one of the daughters drew her forth, "It's
possible you might die tonight?"

After a pause the woman responded, "Yes. It is possible. I
might." She leaned back and returned to sleep.

A few hours later T lay down next to her, as he always did. He
fell sound asleep. In the middle of the night he awoke, aware that
she had moved. He looked. She sat straight up next to him. They
kept a light on in the room. He was accustomed to that, but now
he could see around her a pink glow that brightened to red and
then gold. He had no idea how long this lasted. *"Oh. My God,"* she

said. "There was no fear. It was all very peaceful," he told me several weeks later. After speaking, she lay back down and breathed evenly. T returned to sleep.

At 6 a.m. the daughters came in to administer the next round of medicine. When they opened their mother's mouth, her breath was like air from a refrigerator. "We die in stages," T said. "Perhaps her spirit left when I saw the aura. Her body still had a way to go." She remained immobile throughout the day, never spoke again nor even registered awareness. Late that evening, her body ceased to function.

I had known T and his wife for fifteen years. They were deeply faithful people. Not once in all that time had I heard them speak of "auras" or say anything that indicated they even thought about such matters.

Someone told me that most clergy have a good collection of stories like the one I heard from T. That exaggerates the case, but only slightly. Now and again we hear accounts of the utterly unexpected. The people who speak most credibly are neither religious kooks nor given to fantasy. They call no attention to themselves, nor do they claim any form of spiritual superiority. Many have remained silent for years about what they experienced. When they do share, they do it quietly. "You know, I need to tell you something that once happened to me."

What these persons offer is brief. A few sentences. An account lasting five minutes at most. Bullet points of experience:

- Much to his astonishment, a man started to pray in tongues. The phrase he repeated over and over sounded Middle Eastern, but he had no idea what it meant. He wrote it down phonetically. The next day he shared the phrase with a linguist friend. The friend raised an eyebrow and looked at him. "This means, 'God has cleansed you.'" The man, who knew much guilt, carried those liberating words for years.

- For ten years a small group met for quiet prayer and sharing, once a month, three hours each meeting. Through a long period of silence they opened to God's presence among them. Then they spoke of what was happening in their lives. After that they returned to extended silence. This was all they ever did. Meeting after meeting they found themselves lifted in a manner that lay beyond description.

- A highly educated pastor deeply committed to social justice ministry found herself called on to deal with what she could only describe as "a case of demonic possession and prayer for deliverance." "My heavens, I never thought I'd get involved in anything like that!" In her own words she was "shaken, humbled, and awed" by the experience. Through it all, in ways she could never quite explain, her ministry of social justice grew.

- A man lay dying of pancreatic cancer. For days he bore much pain. One afternoon the doctor told his wife, "It's only a matter of time," by which he meant, "There're just a few hours at most." An hour later the man opened his eyes and said to his wife, "It's so beautiful! It's so beautiful!" He died peacefully a short time later. For decades his widow treasured his words.

The bearers of such tales are invariably amazed by what they have encountered. They attest firmly to what happened but make no claim to understand it. They declare, often quietly, that something real has broken in upon them from beyond the secure boundaries of normal, day-to-day living.

When persons make such a declaration, the story they tell starts to intertwine with our own. Or at least I find this is so for me. I can, of course, dismiss the account. If T had been boastful in telling his experience, if he had in some way been vaunting himself, I would have done just that. When the tones are hushed, though, and the person is as astounded as I am, then I listen.

Beyond listening, I face several choices as to what I do next. I can mentally place a "That's Interesting" label on the event and file it somewhere in the back of my mind where, in truth, it will not receive a lot of attention. I can obsess on the matter, turning it over and over again. If I'm careful about the person's privacy, I can speak of it to others and do some investigating. "Has anybody else here experienced something like this?" Or—and this is ultimately where I am drawn—I can follow a twofold piece of counsel. In part the counsel arises from the long history of religious experience, not only in Christianity but in other faiths as well. In part, and most intimately, the counsel comes from watching T and persons like him. The two elements go together, but I must attend to each.

First, I need to recall that in the strangeness and power of religious experience, we human creatures deal with what is both overwhelming and beyond our grasp. "Religions begin as a slave to mystery not a manifesto of truth," writes Terry Tempest Williams in her supremely thoughtful spiritual autobiography.[1] Religions don't get started because somebody sat down and figured everything out. The primal image is not of the scholar seated at a desk nor of a priest bowing slowly before the altar. It is of Moses whipping off his sandals and hiding his face. It is of a Jewish girl recoiling from an odd figure that suddenly pops in and says, "Hail!" It is of shadowed forms fleeing in terror from an empty tomb.

Rudolf Otto held that anything worthy of the name religion has The Holy at its core. The Holy can be neither comprehended nor controlled. It can meet us and fill us with awe, dread, or bliss beyond any natural comfort. The Hebrews spoke of this abiding core of religion as *qadosh*. The Greeks called it *agios*, the Romans *sacer*. For Buddhists it is a far more vibrant "void" than what the Western meaning of that word allows us to hear.[2] The Holy is as real as our breath, yet when it comes to describing it, Saint Bernard wrote long ago, "I can as little tell of it as I can touch the skies with my finger, or run upon the sea or make a dart stand still in the air."[3]

For years I treasured friendship with an older scientist. He grasped mathematical concepts and theories of particle physics with the same ease that a nine-month-old infant latches onto a rattle. The more he played with what he found, the more he filled

---

1. Williams, *Leap,* 80.
2. Otto, *The Idea of the Holy,* 6–30.
3. Ibid., 34–35.

with wonder. As wonder took hold, he turned his fine, inquiring mind to God and theology. At length, he came to something that both shook and lifted him. "Imagine," he said one day, "trying to teach calculus to an inchworm. Calculus is out there. It's absolutely real. But do you think the inchworm can grasp it?" He leaned back in his chair and relaxed. "We're the inchworm!" he laughed, and then fell silent.

"A God comprehended is no God,"[4] wrote the Reformed theologian Gerhard Tersteegen in the eighteenth century. "Tao can be talked about, but not the Eternal Tao"[5] go the familiar lines the *Tao Teh Ching* offered ages before. With his wonder-filled silence my scientist friend honored an unyielding fact. The Holy lies beyond us all.

As I think on my scientist friend, his humility points me back to T and the further perspective I need to hold close. Time has passed since T saw the aura and heard his wife's words. He long pondered what happened that night. He still does, but he has also moved into fresh ways. What came with such power has deepened him, but he is not preoccupied. The unexplained light and his wife's fearless *"Oh. My God"* remains within him as a quiet, healing gift. Occasionally, when he senses word of his experience might help someone else, he speaks of it.

---

4. Ibid., 25.
5. Wu, *Tao Teh Ching*, 1961.

19

Supplicant

JACK'S VISIT LASTED TEN minutes at most. Monday evening my father had called from a hospital eight hundred miles away to say my mother's brain tumor was inoperable. Twenty-four hours later, the phone rang. "Jack here," said the voice on the other end of the line. "I just heard. May I come over?" I answered, "Yes. Please." Forty-five minutes later Jack hustled through our front door. Not given to formalities, he was even quicker than usual. He nodded to Jean, looked at me. "I'm sorry," he said. He sat down in our front room. We did the same.

"You found out yesterday?" he asked.

"Yes," and I filled him in on the details. Over the weekend we had hope. On Friday preliminary tests put the tumor in a favorable spot. Monday's surgery shattered the hope. "She has two-to-six months."

Jack took a breath. "Do you mind if I, uh?" He didn't finish the sentence. He hunched over in his chair, his hands clasped between his knees, his head thrust downward. The words came slowly. No polish. No effort at eloquence. Just words and long pauses. Both the words and the pauses bore every ounce of energy in him.

"God . . . Help my friend here . . . Help . . .
   . . . his wife . . . Help . . .

his father . . . and his . . . whole . . . family . . .
Help his mother . . . "

That's all I remember. Then came the "Amen." Jack lifted his head. He stood up and sighed. "I'll be in touch," he said. He was out the door and gone.

I had heard him pray in public. It was the same. He strained and pressed. Absolutely everything in him passed through whatever came out. Once in worship at a denominational meeting I sat next to a seasoned pastor whose public prayers rang with balanced phrases and precisely chosen words. His diction was flawless and his honey-toned voice pleasing to everyone within its ample range. Jack had just stood in front of us and battled his way through a prayer for world peace. Head down, he hurried back to his seat. The fellow next to me leaned sideways and, in an uncharacteristic voice, rasped in my ear, "Jack gives the best prayers I've ever heard," to which I answered, "Amen."

Well, Jack had said his "Amen" in our house and was gone. In a real sense, this whole tale was over. The man came. He prayed. That was it. He cared enough to visit us. He lifted our need. What more could I ask? What more can anyone say about the whole situation?

And yet I still contend with questions. Why after so many years is the memory of his prayer that night so vivid? Why in the months that followed did his plain, earnest words become such a channel of grace for us? It was not because my mother lived eleven months instead of six or two. That she lived a little longer offered its own cluster of blessings for her and for us all. Had she died the morning after Jack walked out our door, however, what he brought that night would still have been with us. So what happened in that moment? Why did we feel peace amid the sudden absolute shaking of our world? And why do other people nod in recognition when I tell the story of his halting petition and then quote my friend, "Jack gives the best prayers I ever heard"? Hints have come as I've thought over the years. Some are obvious. Some surprising. Some uncomfortable. The story still unfolds. I am dealing with Jack's un-adorned exposition of the simple, ancient act of prayer.

For one thing, in recent years it has become clear that Jack was doing far more that night than thinking of me and my family. I don't mean to belittle something here. To say "I am thinking of you," as many are fond of doing today, can be a profoundly kind gesture. I don't wish to cast it aside. Truly thinking of someone is a deeply sympathetic act, meaningful both to the one doing the thinking and to those thought of. Jack, though, all but splayed himself on our living room floor.

This was Jack the former All-American athlete, "The Orga-nizer," the only person to appear twice in this collection of tales. This was Jack with his first-rate mind, his encyclopedic knowledge of economic hurts, and his even larger vision of how to meet those hurts. This was Jack whose leadership gave birth to camps for poor kids, health fairs, and clothing centers all across the sparsely popu-lated counties above the Adirondacks.

This was Jack, who had every reason to be confident of himself.

This was Jack begging, pleading, crying out.

God . . . help.

This was Jack reaching into something he could not control.

I am convinced one reason so many today say, "I'm thinking of you," rather than, "I'm praying for you," is that "I'm praying for you" has become cheap. It is too often a toss-off line, an easy bit of comfort, void of investment, divorced from struggle, and hence empty of meaning. Genuine thinking engages the whole person. And here was Jack totally engaged. Yet he wasn't just tussling with his own thoughts or working over his own finely honed ideas. Nor did he reach out with his mind in some effort to touch my grief or ease my father's anguish or lessen my mother's pain, as com-passionate as these gestures would have been. Jack had gathered to himself all the grief, the anguish, the pain of that moment and then, still bearing these, he wrestled with some great Immensity beyond him.

The names for the Immensity he approached stretch beyond number. El Shaddai. Elohim. Yahweh. Allah. Abba. Sophia. Shiva. The Holy. The Everlasting One. The Power Greater than Ourselves. Islam holds ninety-nine sacred names for God in part as a sign that no end of names exists and all the names we come up with will never enfold all that God is. Even adjectives of location fail. Is God "out there"? Does God lie "deep within"? Mystics tell us these distinctions finally vanish. Jack was not just thinking that night. He struggled with the Immensity that utterly exceeded his grasp and was overwhelmingly real.

As I have thought on Jack praying that night, I have come to see his unguarded genuineness. Psychologist Eugene Minkowski noted the absolute necessity of sincerity in prayer: "Prayer cannot *not* be sincere; otherwise it is not prayer."[1] Jack acted without calculation, purified of worry over what others thought or how he sounded. No frills. No concern for eloquence. All that mattered for Jack was our need and where he turned.

I recall Jack that night and I see both surrender and dependence. Neither is popular in our culture. It is far more admirable to stand on our own two feet. It is more appealing to act with clear, rational justification for what we do. Or if that is not possible, at least we can pretend. Jack's prayer that night rested on a far different foundation. This foundation said, "I do not fully know you, God, and I cannot. But you are real. We are in need. Hear our cry!"

And as I have reflected on Jack over the years, I have come to see how fully he was shaped by what he prayed to. A few years ago I read an enthusiastic treatment of prayer. Its author claimed it doesn't matter what we pray to. We can turn to Jesus, Spider Woman, whatever. With the right mindset, the writer said, the effects will be the same. Something about this did not square with what I had seen in Jack. Nor did it square with much else. Spider Woman may have her strengths, but if, for instance, Johann Sebastian Bach had prayed to her devoutly every day for a quarter-century, I doubt that even after that amount of time she would have inspired him to write the B Minor Mass.

1. Minkowski, *Lived Time*, 106.

"Prayer is a two-way conversation," an elderly nun once told me. "If the conversation goes deep enough, we are molded by the One we pray to." John of the Cross wrote that if in prayer we gaze on the fire of God's love, we ourselves begin to burn with that fire.[2] Jack prayed to the Living God who weeps for our brokenness and cares for the poor. This had everything to do with why he cared so deeply for the poor and spent decades meetings needs which others rarely noticed. It was why he came through the door that night to be with Jean and me in our brokenness. He had been infused by the God he prayed to. The all-consuming fire burned within him.

When I think on that night he came and prayed with us, I am finally caught by where Jack's prayer carried us. It drew us, and we let ourselves be drawn, into a realm beyond us. When Jack left, what we had encountered remained with us. Our sadness had not gone. Weeping and change still lay ahead. The horizon of our thoughts, however, had been stretched. A Presence embraced us. Examining his own experience of prayer, Eugene Minkowski noted that prayer led him to a horizon "so far that it seems to be outside time and space while wholly embodying them."[3] There he discovered "an inexhaustible source of new forces, a source which can neither change nor even less give out." Through prayer, he said, "we touch the absolute."[4]

Jack put it his own way when he left that night, head down, hurrying out, uttering barely a word. In our presence, he had dared approach the Holy.

---

2. John of the Cross, *The Living Flame of Love,* 162.

3. Minkowski, *Lived Time,* 105–106.

4. Ibid., 110.

20

The Theologian

I FOUND HER AN enigma. Not that anything negative about the woman crossed my mind. Quite the contrary. Though I needed an interpreter to grasp her words, her intellect and warmth required no translation. These glowed whether she stood in front of several hundred people or talked one-to-one. And from the start, I saw the esteem with which others regarded her. I knew that this response related to the office she held. She served as regional administrator for a large number of Colombian Presbyterian churches, and that role itself commanded respect. Even so, I puzzled increasingly as our weeks together passed by. Why did her smile radiate such energy? How did she manage to connect so deeply with others whether they were educated like herself or *campesinos* who had been driven from the land? Most persistently, why did this Gloria command such authority? On these matters I reached for something I could not name. The answer emerged only after I returned to the United States and had time to reflect on a cross made of shoes, her hands, and an alliance of love.

The Cross Made of Shoes

"Everybody! Make a cross on the floor with your shoes!" called Gloria. "And only one shoe from each of you. We'll never fit it in if you use both!" She stood before two hundred Colombian women packed into the small sanctuary of a church in Barranquilla. They had gathered from across the city and many hours away to observe the International Day of the Woman. Responding to Gloria's instruction the entire group laughed and squished forward. They were of African, Indigenous, and European heritage, tiny and strong, tall and willowy, honey colored, leather, black. Many young. Many old. Just as many in between. All one body now, they surged ahead, placing their shoes.

The lone male, I sat. Two women spotted me, laughed, and waved me forward. Out of habit I took off both shoes. "Uno!" one called. I joined the crush. All of us laughed now. And then as we finished, quiet settled. We looked. A cross spread before us. A cross made of work shoes, high heels, and dusty sandals.

We went back to our chairs. Gloria read Luke 8:40–56. Smiling, and with few words, she noted the passage spoke of two women, one well provided for, the other drained of her resources, both in pain. She passed out questions that dealt with the pain in women's lives, with Jesus' healing response to the women in the passage, and with the response women can make to the pain of others around them. Gloria invited the women to circle their chairs in groups of six and discuss the scripture passage and the questions.

Translation at this point, particularly for a male, would have invaded something private. For forty minutes I sat in a corner and absorbed the sounds of earnest discussion. Occasionally laughter broke out. A few groups moved into prayer, then back to discussion. No one got up to mill about. None looked around with an expression that said, "We're done. How about the rest of you?"

Gloria stood and asked that one person from each group share how they had responded to the questions. This phase lasted another thirty minutes. Again, no one moved about or even fidgeted. Mostly the very young reported. Concise and with passion they spoke of brokenness in people's lives and of the call to heal that brokenness.

After this sharing the singing began. Joyful songs and plaintive. Some soft, some loud enough to echo through streets twisting far beyond the church. Arms waved in the air. One woman dressed as John Calvin, beard and all, appeared briefly. Calvin said he wasn't quite sure what the women were up to, but they sounded good and he told them to keep at it. The women laughed. The aroma of tamales drifted in from a room just beyond the sanctuary. The women sang two quieter songs.

Gloria, who had been out of sight, stepped forward and stood by the cross made of shoes. With eyes that touched on everyone in the room, she spoke of Jesus. Jesus had come to heal our brokenness. He had healed the pain of two women, one rich, one poor. He was here for everybody. He invited us to know his healing in our own lives and to take that healing back into the world around us.

Gloria motioned for us to reclaim our shoes.

We pressed close, limped, laughed, and supported one another, a single body about to fan out through the city and along the entire northern coast of Colombia. With help from two other members of that cross-formed body, I found my muddy black walker. I laced it, stood up, and looked for Gloria. She had disappeared into the room where women were fixing tamales.

Her Hands

Seven of us sat around a table in the small conference room next to Gloria's office. Gloria, presiding, sat at one end. Next to her and slightly back from the table, a seminary student leaned forward, his hands in his lap. My co-worker, Ruth Noel, and I pressed against one side of the table, my head tilted to catch Ruth's translation. At the far end perched Gloria's colleague, another minister. Opposite Ruth and me sat two men from a camp for *displacazados*, persons displaced by Colombia's internal conflict. The older of the two was tall and muscular. He wore a t-shirt proclaiming Colombia as first in the world for the victims of anti-personnel mines. The younger sported a red polo shirt. He was short but as muscular as his towering partner.

The younger man was trying to help people organize a school in their ill-equipped camp. His heart was in the task, but he needed coaching. Gloria was his mentor. Her education could have intimidated him, likewise her position and wide reputation. Seeking counsel from any woman might easily have become a source of humiliation. None of this happened.

Gloria asked questions. Was the man working with his board of *displacazados* and not trying to do everything by himself? He was working alone. Gloria noted ways to involve others. Did he know it was important to contact the Secretary of Education? Yes, but he had not done that. He was not sure he could contact the Secretary without her permission. "You can do things without my permission and without the permission of our churches. What you do won't affect our support." Did he remember he could call her and she would be willing to phone the Education Office and put in a word? That might open some doors. Yes, he remembered.

As the conversation continued, I became aware of Gloria's hands. Whether at rest or gesturing, her palms opened outward. They remained open through the most pointed suggestions she had to offer. She was receiving from the man even as she spoke.

In time I learned that those hands had opened in vastly different settings. Or more to the point, Gloria's spirit, as mirrored in her hands, had widened to catch the grace and goodness that came from any with whom she spoke. In parishes and classrooms, at the university where she had long served as chaplain, in barrios of the poor, and on the farms of campesinos, she persistently received on some deep and fundamental level. As she did this, an unspoken "*Gracias*" moved from her to any with whom she conversed.

The man in the red shirt left the meeting with erect posture and a firm handclasp for everyone.

The New Alliance of Love

Gloria stood in front of a packed congregation. The drums and guitars had just faded in this, the most charismatic church I visited in Barranquilla. She began matter-of-factly, as she always did. The crowd grew still.

"I want to talk to you today about the New Alliance of Love. We're now at the fifth Sunday of Lent. In these forty days we see the New Alliance that Jesus is making. He gives us a whole new ethic of love. He draws us into relation with God and gives us a completely new way of relating to the world around us."

As I later went over my notes and found the word "ethic" I recalled something a professor of mine once said about the New England divine Jonathan Edwards: "He talked concepts, not mush. Ordinary folk hung on every word for hours." Gloria didn't push into the hours, but she held with concepts and every head in that room stayed with her.

Gloria pointed to the lesson for the morning. In John 12:20–33 some Greeks wanted to know Jesus. What did Jesus do? "He did not turn them away. This was unbelievable for his culture! His people wanted nothing to do with the Greeks, but he broadened the community. His alliance is for all nations!"

"And yet," Gloria said, "there was something strange. Jesus included the Greeks by pointing to his death. Membership in the New Alliance of Love costs everything. This is a great paradox: the New Alliance brings life in its fullest, but those who wish to be part of that Alliance must be willing to give up everything."

Gloria shared three stories to demonstrate what the New Alliance of Love is really like. She spoke first of a European woman who went to Palestine. The woman was just twenty-three, a beautiful, brilliant student deeply committed to non-violence. One day she tried to stop a Caterpillar from demolishing an innocent family's home. Gloria saw the video. It was difficult to watch. The machine went right over her. Hers was the testimony of youth. She gave her life for what she believed in. She was part of the Alliance.

Gloria told of a Colombian farmer in his seventies who had been driven from his land by armed men. After three years, he returned to his farm and found it fallow. He went to churches, to international organizations, to any who would listen. Would they provide funds so he and others could reclaim and replant the farms they had lost? Support came. The farmers returned to their land. Not long afterward the attacks began all over again. Surrounded by death threats from the guerillas on one side and para-militaries on the other, the man keeps on. All he seeks is the opportunity for people to work the land in peace. He is a member of the New Alliance of Love.

Gloria turned to two persons worshiping with the congregation that day. Any pastor knows this can be a dangerous move. Petty jealousies may ignite and clouds of incredulity smother the illustration. Gloria chose well and this did not happen. Through many years the two had responded to the needs of others. They had given generously, even sacrificed financially. And now, despite personal danger, they were speaking for the dispossessed in Colombia. They had joined Jesus' Alliance of Love.

The sermon ended swiftly. The New Alliance costs, Gloria reminded us. It cost the young woman who went to Palestine, the old man who returned to the land, and was costing people in our midst. It surely cost Jesus. The Alliance is for the God-infected, the God-carriers. It is for folk willing to set Jesus' world-healing love ahead of all else, even if it means carrying the cross.

"Will you," Gloria asked, "be a part of the New Alliance of Love?"

Her Hands

Not until our last night in Colombia did Ruth and I hear Gloria refer to the danger she lived with. Even then the mention was oblique. It arose along the edge of our conversation and quickly passed.

Gloria and another pastor from the Presbytery had taken us out to dinner to thank us for our time in Colombia. One small duty Ruth and I had during our five weeks as accompaniers of the Presbyterian Church in Colombia consisted of spending some time each day sitting in the outer room of the Presbytery Office where Gloria and several others worked. Between the main course and a final cup of coffee, Gloria broke off whatever it was we were talking about and said, "I want you to know, every day when I come into the office, I thank God that you will be out there."

That was the end of it. Behind Gloria's earnestness, though, lay important matters. Until the program we were a part of began, Gloria's office had been under surveillance by the government. This clearly was an act of intimidation designed to stop Presbyterian Churches from speaking out on behalf of the *displazados*. Somehow the presence of *gringos* caused the government to pull back. More immediate, and more threatening, Colombia's President had recently declared that advocates and organizers of the poor were guerilla sympathizers. Such persons were harassed and subject to death threats. Gloria, we knew, was an outspoken advocate for Colombia's four million *displacadazos*. So was the neatly dressed woman pastor seated beside her. Despite the worsening political climate neither would abandon what she was about.

The two women turned to discussing a colleague. He had received numerous threats and, with his family, had been out of the country for two years. In another three months he would return. They feared for his life.

A waiter arrived with coffee. Gloria asked after our early departure and flight across the Caribbean the next day.

I remember nothing of Gloria's hands during the meal. At the end of the evening, though, when she dropped us back at the university where we were staying, those hands gripped our own with astonishing strength. "Thank you for accompanying us," and we felt the "*¡Gracias!*" so many had come to know in her presence.

The Cross Made of Shoes

Somewhere that cross made of shoes is still forming. It no longer holds the tight shape of two crossbars. It has spread through city streets and along country roads, worked its way into office buildings, fine apartments, and simple huts. Yet through all the changes it is still a cross. It marks the presence of a courageous, holy Alliance of Love in a land that desperately needs the Alliance.

One of Gloria's shoes made up a part of that cross the afternoon it came together. "Just a tiny part, that's all, nothing more," Gloria would say. I have no idea where that tiny part of the cross has journeyed since, nor do I have any idea where Gloria is right now. I am sure that wherever shoes and life have taken her, she has gone forth open-handed, ready to receive all that she encounters.

And so I pondered after I got home, "Why does this woman connect so deeply and command such authority?" The answer emerged bit-by-bit and, though unexpected, it did not surprise me when it came. I recalled one day something Sjoren Kierkegaard wrote near the end of one of his thickest volumes: "one does not prepare oneself to become attentive to Christianity by reading books . . . but by immersing oneself deeper in existence."[1] Gloria has immersed herself in the life around her. She has done so in all manner of circumstances. When I think on her and on the wondering her presence raised within me, the word that comes to mind now is "theologian." For some that word may call up images of a person who uses arcane vocabulary and labors in isolation. At root, however, the theologian is a far more compelling figure. In ancient Greece, the theologian told of the gods. In Christianity, the theologian perpetually probes and imparts the essential things of God. Those that do this most compellingly know intimately all the hurt, all the pain, and all the surging grace around them. When Gloria speaks, she speaks out of her immersion in the life that surrounds her and from her unwavering fidelity to the One whose New Alliance of Love demands everything she has. For these reasons she commands authority, and even people who have known her only briefly still remember.

1. Kierkegaard, *Concluding Unscientific Postscript*, 497.

21

"I am so thankful."

WE SAID ALMOST NOTHING during our visit. He heard me enter his multi-bed ward and opened his eyes but did not turn his head. I sat down next to the bed. He nodded, but was too weak to speak. His eyes shut again. I let him know that I would be there for a little while.

He lay amid a tangle of tubes and wires. The monitor at the head of the bed charted unsteady heartbeats.

He was fifty-eight.

"I should have died thirty-four years ago when the thing first hit me," he said while we were just getting acquainted some months before. He had served in the South Pacific during World War II. A fever laid him low for weeks. When it left the doctors told him that he had a severely damaged heart. "Should have died, but I didn't." As he repeated the words a smile broke around the corners of his mouth. His eyebrows shot up sending creases to the top of his forehead.

The first time I had seen him he was dressed in his Sunday best, leaning on his wife's arm, barely able to walk. "He's getting over one of his bouts," his wife told me as the two made their way into a potluck where he sat with the grandkids, ate little but smiled a lot and greeted friends. Over the next months he grew stronger.

He got back to walking on his own. He even picked up a little speed. Then one morning his wife called, "He's had another bout."

He had gone back into what he called "my home away from home," an aging VA hospital twenty miles down a canyon and another ten out on the prairie. For two weeks he steadily got worse. I knew before I saw him that this visit could well be our last. I took his hand that afternoon and prayed with him before leaving.

After the Amen, he spoke his first words of the day: "I am so thankful." He was too weak for any volume, but he said each word distinctly.

"I . . . am . . . so . . . thankful." He repeated himself and opened his eyes wide.

I could not see what he looked on as he spoke. Was it some mind-held scene of the two grandsons and one granddaughter who years later stretched into the keen minded adults everyone knew they would be? Was it all the years of life he never should have had? Or did he see the nurse he mustered enough courage to ask for a date after his fever left? She had glared at him and said, "If you come back and ask me when you're sober I might say 'Yes.'" So he dried out and went back twenty-four hours later. That time she said, "Yes." They got married ten weeks later and had been laughing together ever since. Was he thankful for his years at the mine office where he kept records straight and talked with everybody that came in? Or did he see he'd gotten through another winter and the air was warm and the pasque flowers were flashing purple all across the prairie?

"I am so thankful." He spoke again, his voice as weak as before but each word pulsed with passion. His eyes went shut. He appeared to keep looking.

What was he seeing? Warmth radiated from that eyelid-sheltered gaze. "Love existed before heaven or earth," wrote Hāfiz." "Love's presence is not from our time."[1] Was he gazing on something he had just begun to know in all those years with his wife and children and grandchildren, with co-workers and church friends and spring breezes tumbling down the mountainside? The First

1. Fedeler and Fedeler, *Love's Alchemy,* v.

Letter of John declares: "everyone who loves is born of God and knows God."[2] Did he in that moment view some beckoning vastness and was he entering more fully what he saw? I could not tell what his infinitely expanding heart embraced, but clearly he was held by it.

All was quiet now.

He had relaxed. He lay motionless except for occasional, shallow breaths.

I pressed his hands and said, "Thank you."

A short while later I drove back up the canyon, profoundly grateful for whatever vision of grace this quiet, gentle man had so clearly seen.

---

2. 1 John 4:7b.

Questions for Personal and Group Reflection

FOR EACH INDIVIDUAL STORY readers may wish to consider:

1. If I could ask one question of the central figure in this story, what would it be?

2. What intrigues me about this person? . . . or attracts me? . . . or what do I most admire?

3. What, if anything, am I in tension with as I reflect on this person? Is there anything I would like to challenge? Is there something I wonder about?

4. If I could mimic one element in this person's life, what would it be?

5. Does the central figure in this story remind me of some other person? If so, what is that person's story? What are the details, struggles, delights I remember? What impact did this person have on me?

6. What do I give thanks for in the central figure of this story?

7. Does the narrator of this story express any opinions or thoughts that I disagree with, or agree with, or am in dialogue with?

Questions to reflect on after reading several of the stories

1. In the stories I have read, which person or persons have I most responded to? Why?

2. As different as the persons in these stories are, what do they hold in common?

3. In what differing ways do the people in these stories know God?

4. What unknowns, uncertainties, or pains are persons living with in any of these stories?

5. What certainties or solid touchstones are any of these persons living with?

6. Jesus said, "I am come that they may have life, and have it abundantly." (John 10:10) In what specific ways is life abundant for each of the persons whose story I have read?

7. Some of the persons in these stories are marginalized. What do they show about the needs of the marginalized? . . . about their resilience? . . . about the gifts they have to offer?

Patterns to help people develop an ongoing awareness of their own sacred stories and the stories of others around them

1. *In classes and on retreats* a simple, three movement pattern can help participants move beyond the stories on the page and become more aware of their own stories and the stories of others.

   - Begin by focusing on the story in the book. Draw on the questions noted above and any other questions that arise from the group.

   - Then invite participants to spend time in quietness reflecting on:

     a. Who does this remind me of? What was that person like? What effect did this person have on me? What do I give thanks for in this person?

    b. What about my own story? Where have I experienced what the central figure in this story experienced, or done what this person has done?

- Finally, drawing the group back together, invite each person to share the stories that came to them, both as they thought of others and as they thought about themselves.

2. *Live with a question through the week. Then do it again, and again, and again.* Physician and writer Rachel Naomi Remen once observed, "An unanswered question is a fine traveling companion. It sharpens your eye for the road."[1] Carry a single question through a week, such as: "This week, whose faith story moved me, even if they never spoke that story out loud but simply lived it?" or "Where this week have I seen someone whose authentically lived faith has spoken to me?" or "This week, where has my own faith story entered new territory, or reentered old territory for fresh exploration?" or "Where have I experienced the Holy this week? Where have I known God?" Take just one of these questions, or one like them. Live with the question for a week. Pause to reflect on it, particularly near the end of the week. Then live with it again for the week after that, and again for the week after that. Rachel Naomi Remen was right. Persons who follow this practice soon discover they are growing more alive to what has been there all along in the lives of others and in their own.

3. *Develop the habit of unhurried, expectant attentiveness to the stories of others and to your own.* We may be able to name swiftly the people whose stories have enriched us. To recall them fully, though, we need to take time, allowing images, sayings, and whole incidents to surface and claim us once again. Similarly, it takes little time to list important elements in our personal stories, but to value fully the richness of our own narrative and how God has met us there we need to let the full recollections appear and savor them as they come. Quietness on retreat, in a classroom, and simply when we are

---

1. Remen, *Kitchen Table Wisdom,* 293.

alone provides unhurried time for stories to emerge, enrich us, and draw us into still greater awareness of holiness all around us.

Bibliography

Abbot, Edwin A. *Flatland: A Romance of Many Dimensions.* New York. Dover, 1992.

Augustine of Hippo. *Basic Writings of Saint Augustine, vol. 1.* New York: Random, 1948.

Bruteau, Beatrice. *God's Ecstasy.* New York: Crossroad, 1997.

Buber, Martin. *I and Thou.* New York: Charles Scribner's Sons, 1958.

Fideler, David and Sabrineh Fideler, translators. *Love's Alchemy: Poems from the Sufi Tradition.* Novato, CA: New World Library, 2006

Gardner, Helen, ed. *The Metaphysical Poets.* Baltimore: Penguin, 1957.

Gingerich, Owen. *God's Universe.* Cambridge, MA: Belknap of Harvard University Press, 2006.

Haring, Bernard. *A Sacramental Spirituality.* New York: Shed & Ward, 1965.

Hillman, James. *The Force of Character and the Lasting Life.* New York: Random House, 1999.

Hopkins, Gerard Manley. *Gerard Manley Hopkins: A Selection of His Poems and Prose by W. H. Gardner.* London: Penguin, 1953.

Hulme, T. E. *Speculations: Essays on Humanism and the Philosophy of Art.* London: Routledge & Kegan Paul, 1936.

John of the Cross. *The Dark Night of the Soul & The Living Flame of Love.* Glasgow, Great Brittan: Harper Collins, 1995.

Lanier, Jaron. "Raft to the Future: How Time Emerges from Math," *Discover Magazine* (October 2006). http://discovermagazine.com/2006/oct/jarons-world-raft-future.

Lopez, Barry. *Crow and Weasel.* San Francisco: North Point, 1980.

Kierkegaard, Sjoren. *Concluding Unscientific Postscript.* Translated by David F. Swensen. Princeton, NJ: Princeton University Press, 1941.

Minkowski, Eugene. *Lived Time: Phenomenological and Psychopathological Studies.* Evanston, IL: Northwestern University Press, 1970.

Otto, Rudolf. *The Idea of the Holy.* New York: Galaxy Book of Oxford University Press, 1958.

Prang, Sebastian. "The Tiles of Infinity." *Saudi Aramco World,* September–October 2009, 24–31.

Raymo, Chet. *Skeptics and True Believers: The Exhilarating Connection between Science and Religion.* New York: Walker, 1998.

Remen, Rachel Naomi. *Kitchen Table Wisdom: Stories that Heal.* New York: Riverhead, 1996.

Seasoltz, R. Kevin. "One House, Many dwellings: Open and Closed Communion." *Worship* 75.9 (September 2009), 419.

Sih, Paul K. T., ed. *Tao Teh Ching.* Translated by Wu, John H. C. New York: St. John's University Press, 1961.

Stace, W. T. *Time and Eternity: An Essay in the Philosophy of Religion.* Princeton, NJ: Princeton University Press, 1952.

Steinhart, Arnold. *Violin Dreams.* New York: Houghton Mifflin, 2006.

Wedel, Mark. "Bach Festival Artists Deliver Powerful Mozart Requiem." In *Kalamazoo Gazette, Arts and Entertainment,* May 22, 2006.

Williams, Terry Tempest. *Leap.* New York: Pantheon, 2000.